The Blind Loon: A Bestiary

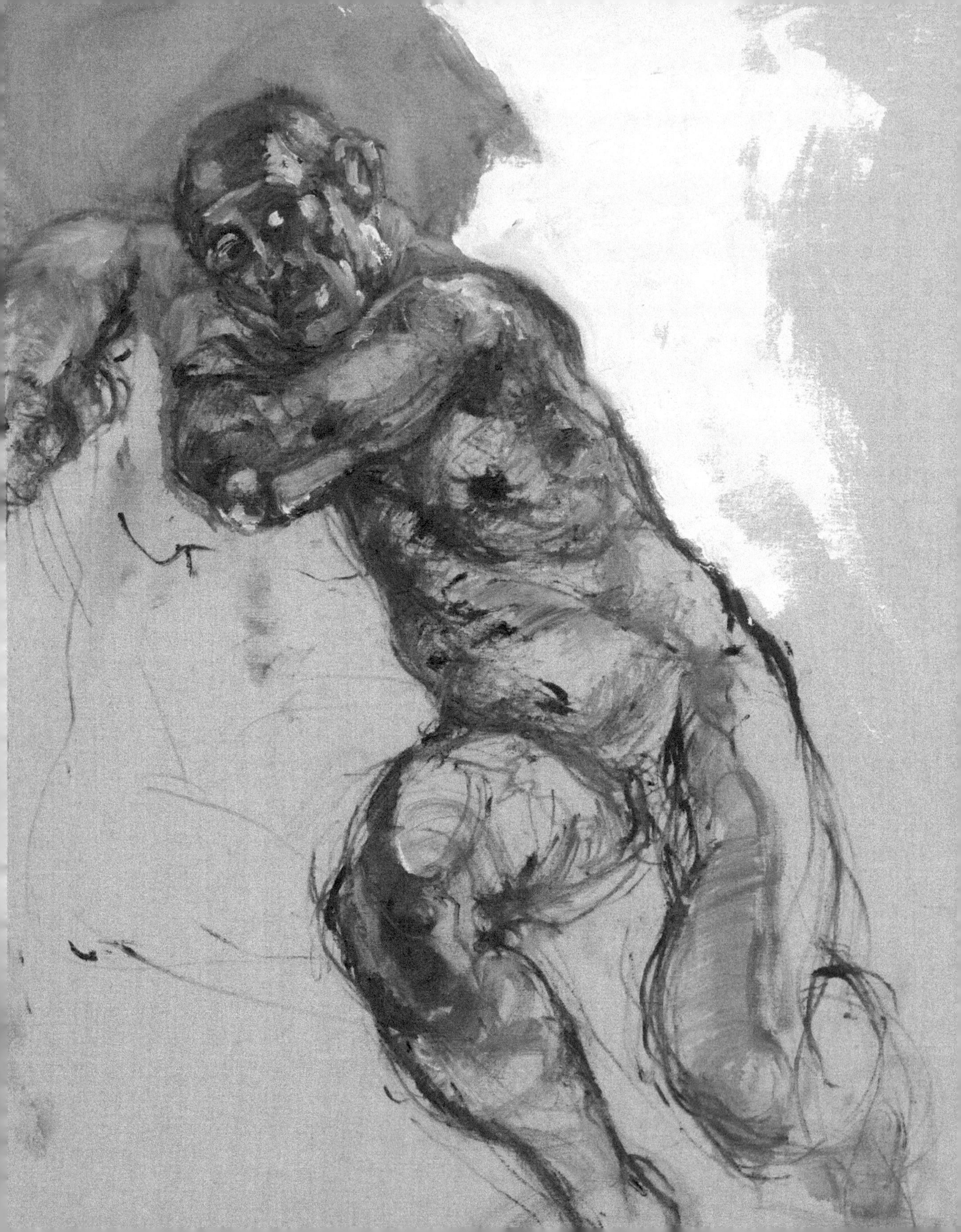

THE BLIND LOON
a bestiary

WRITTEN BY
Ed Shacklee

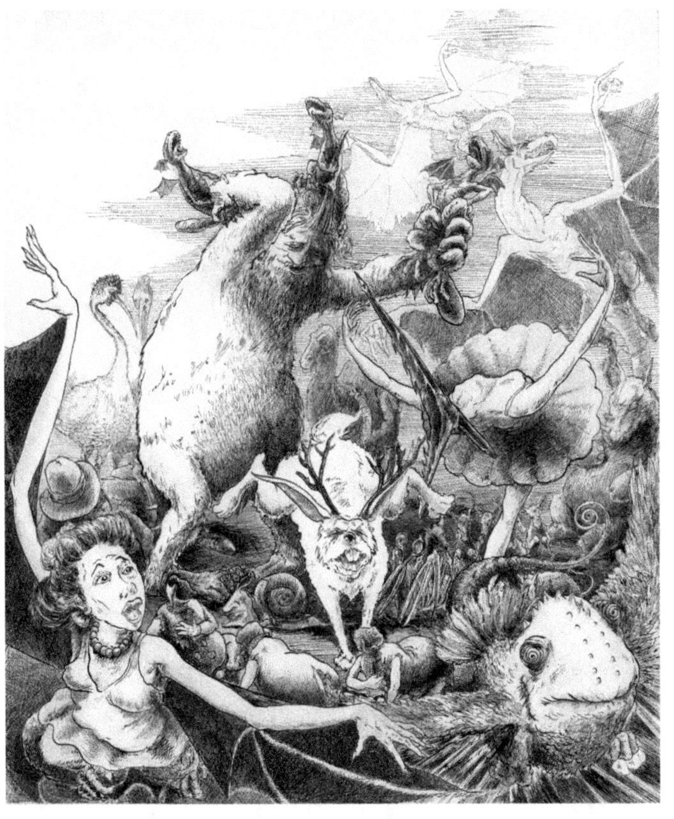

ILLUSTRATED BY
Russ Spitkovsky

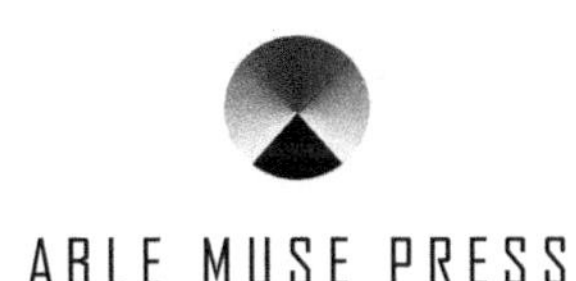

ABLE MUSE PRESS

First published in 2017 by

Able Muse Press

www.ablemusepress.com

Printed in the United States of America

Library of Congress Control Number: 2017930327

ISBN 978-1-927409-87-9 (paperback)
ISBN 978-1-77349-004-5 (hardcover)
ISBN 978-1-927409-86-2 (digital)

Front- and back-cover image, and book illustrations, by Russ Spitkovsky

Cover & book design by Alexander Pepple

Able Muse Press is an imprint of *Able Muse:* A Review of Poetry, Prose & Art—at www.ablemuse.com

Able Muse Press
467 Saratoga Avenue #602
San Jose, CA 95129

Acknowledgments

I am grateful to the editors of the following journals where many of the poems in this collection originally appeared, sometimes in earlier versions:

Able Muse: "Memoirs of the Widow Mantis" and "Song of the Blind Loon"

Angle: "The Camel," "Darwin's Monkey," "The Friend," "Great White Hunters," "The Heart," "The Imaginary Friend," "The Inkling," "The Jackalope," "The Lesser Pundit," "The Otter," "The Pleasant," "A Pry of Gossips," "The Rabbit in the Hat," "The Snipe," "The Snub," and "The Tortoise"

The Asses of Parnassus: "Chimera" and "The Crocodile"

Autumn Sky Poetry Daily: "The Carrion Flamingo," "If Wishes Were Horses," "Let Down Your Hair," "The Mole People," and "A Riposte of Gibes"

The British Fantasy Society Journal: "Prey of the Lamia"

Calamaro: "Monkey Manqué"

Goreyesque: "The Beast in the Jungle," "The Camelopard," "The Gilded Void," "The Kraken," and "Worms in the End"

Innisfree Poetry Journal: "The Stalking Horse"

Kin Poetry Journal: "Butterfly Collection," "The Dodos," "Loch Ness," "The Ostrich," and "The Rhinoceros"

Light: "The Common Retronaut," "Balloon Animal," "The Cat's Meow," "The Flea Circus," "A Fog of Blurbs," "The Mope," "The Prim," "The Satyr," "A Schism of Zebras," "The Snide," and "A Zaftig of Hippos"

Lighten Up Online: "An Aloofness of Snoots," "The Antelope," "The Flowering of Noon," "The Logorrhea," "The Moaning of Life," "The Terrible Beauty," and "The Wyvern"

Loch Raven Review: "Spider on a Pillow"

Lucid Rhythms: "The Gift Horse"

The New Verse News: "The Golden Calf"

Per Contra: "Making a Monkey" and "The Winged Boy"

Rat's Ass Review: "The Ravenous Dream"

Rattle: "So We Beat Them"

The Road Not Taken: "The Python"

Shot Glass Journal: "Faith" and "Sheep Is the Past Tense of Wolf"

Snakeskin: "The Doppelgänger," "The Melodious Sappho," "A Now of Hipsters," "Pod People," and "The Sloth"

SteinbeckNow: "The Ankylosaurus," "I Am What I Am," "A Joust of Narwhals," and "The Slink"

String Poet: "The Horse of a Different Color"

Strong Verse: "The Night Circus"

I would also like to thank Kema Larsen, my childhood's end; Cally Conan-Davies, my undefeated blue; Sean Brebbia, my pint of courage; Maddie and Mae Brebbia, my pirates; David Mason, my cockatoo; Susan de Sola, my interpreter of mimes; Richard Meyer, my timely arrow; and especially Martha Jean and Joseph C. Shacklee, my beloved parents.

I dedicate this book to the memory of Mabel E. Mullikin.

Contents

The Blind Loon: A Bestiary

Now with my father's favors, the lute and skill,
Through the dark smelly places where the gods play
With the unlucky, I ape a smiling way,
Working prodigious feats of vaudeville.

— William Meredith, from "Orpheus"

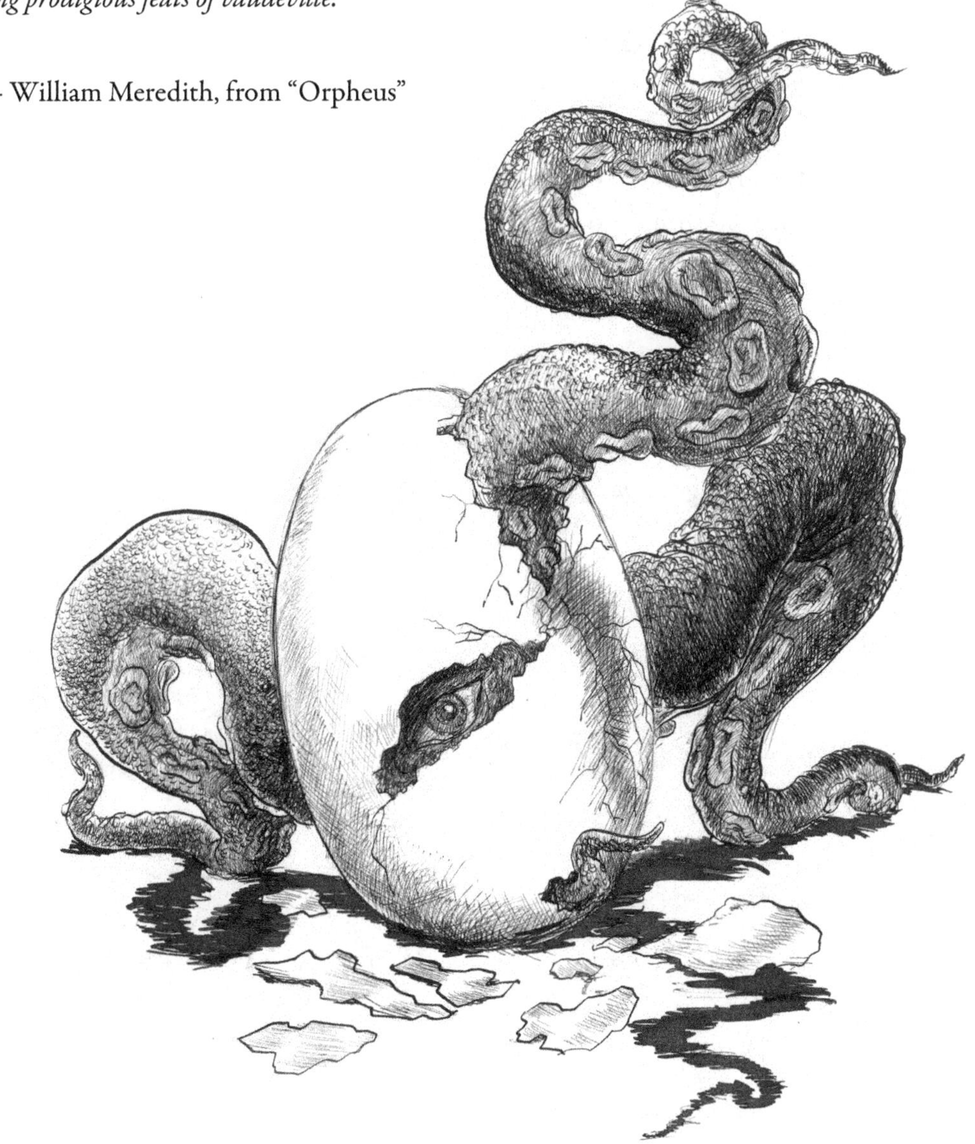

Faith

The crow did not come back,
and Noah, in a crush of paired beasts,
turned to the dove, the peace bringer,
let it go;

the myriad reduced to doubles,
the ship shrunk to a pistachio shell,
the sullen, swollen sea so pearly gray,
so silent.

Now that is faith, said the rats,
their eyes like black bits of diamond
in the bilge, *to believe there are only
two of us.*

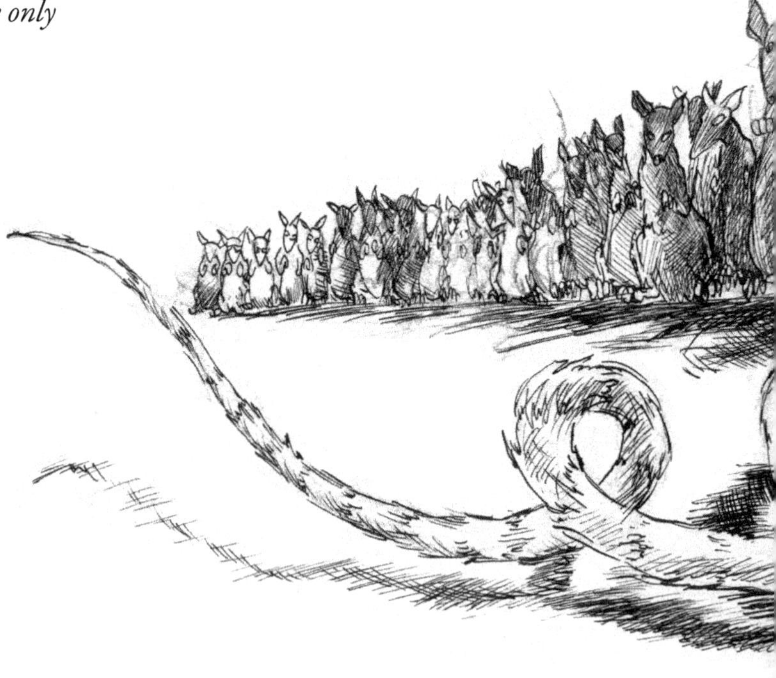

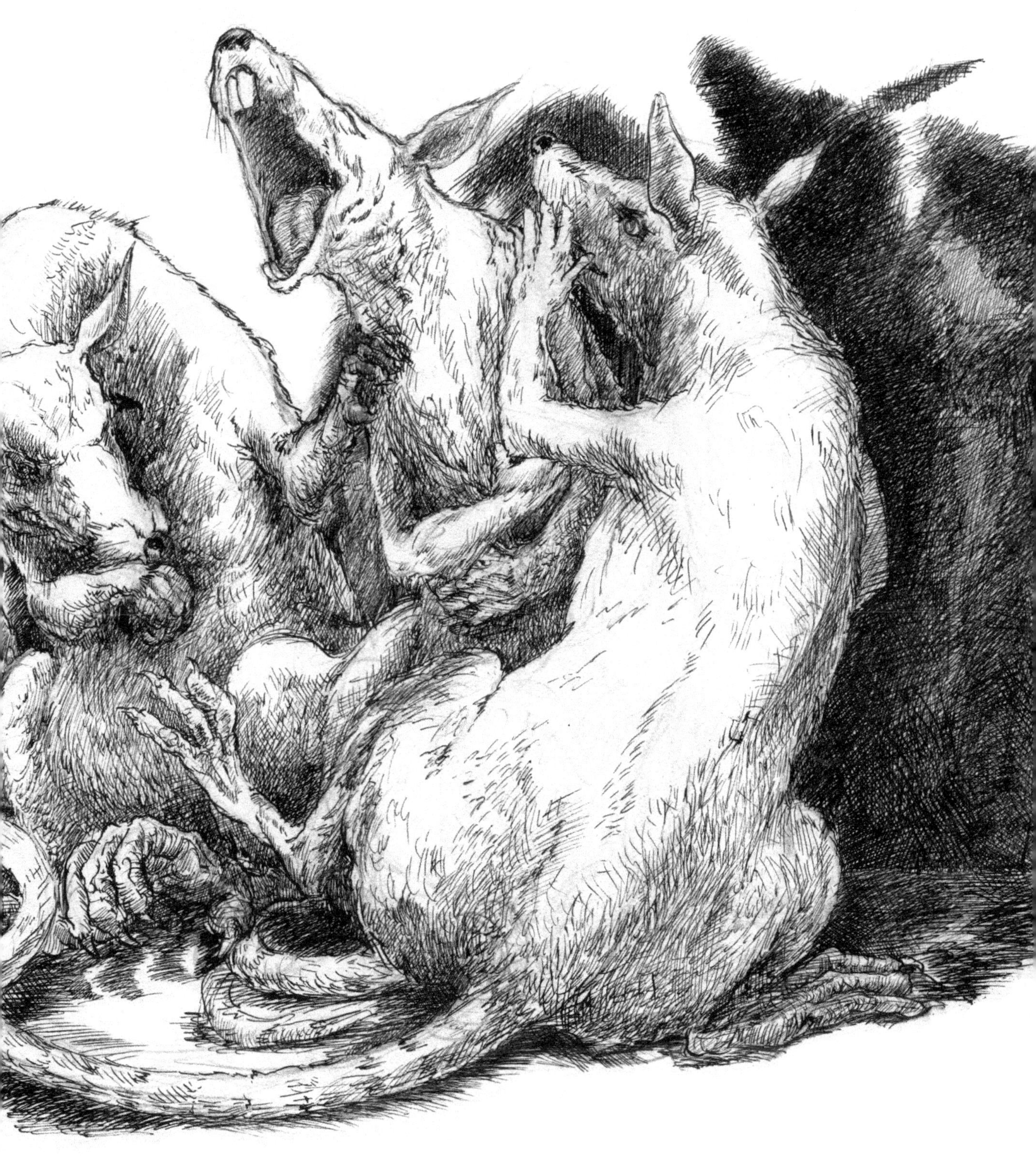

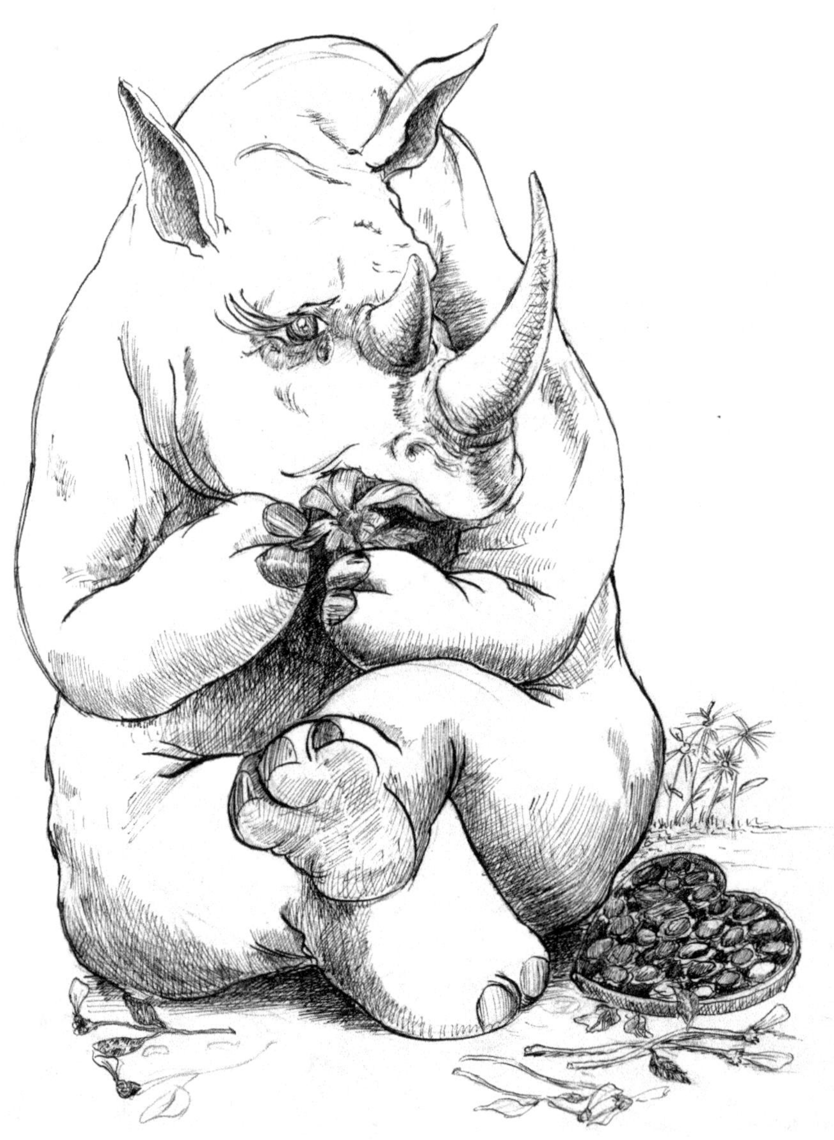

The Rhinoceros

The rhino is a gentle sort
who's locked his heart inside a fort,
a clumsy, quadrupedal yurt,
afraid he'll get his feelings hurt.

Yet deep within that horny hide
he courts an extroverted side,
and—though near-sighted—hopes to find
a love whose love is almost blind.

Armored, amorous, wide of hip,
as gray as any battleship,
desire bursting at the seams,
he roams the veldt, alone, and dreams

he'll bump into his dreams distilled, a
heavy date, his own Brunhilda.

The Mope

Drear and friendless, fear the endless droning of the Mope,
whose septic, soft dyspeptic fretting's epic in its scope.
Its swinging moods are dreadful, like a dead man on a rope.

Disdaining food for thought, it spots the snot in the sonata,
the rat in five-star ratings, not itself until it's got a
little cross to bear or else a prominent stigmata.

Insipid, uninspired, far too tired for a tirade,
its spine is wet spaghetti, and its final nerve is frayed.
Its sobs are often stifled but a trifle overplayed

as foresight warns, then hindsight mourns: it looks within, and sighs
a small, resigned lamenting sound, like heat escaping pies,
yet may not bore you with details, although Lord knows it tries.

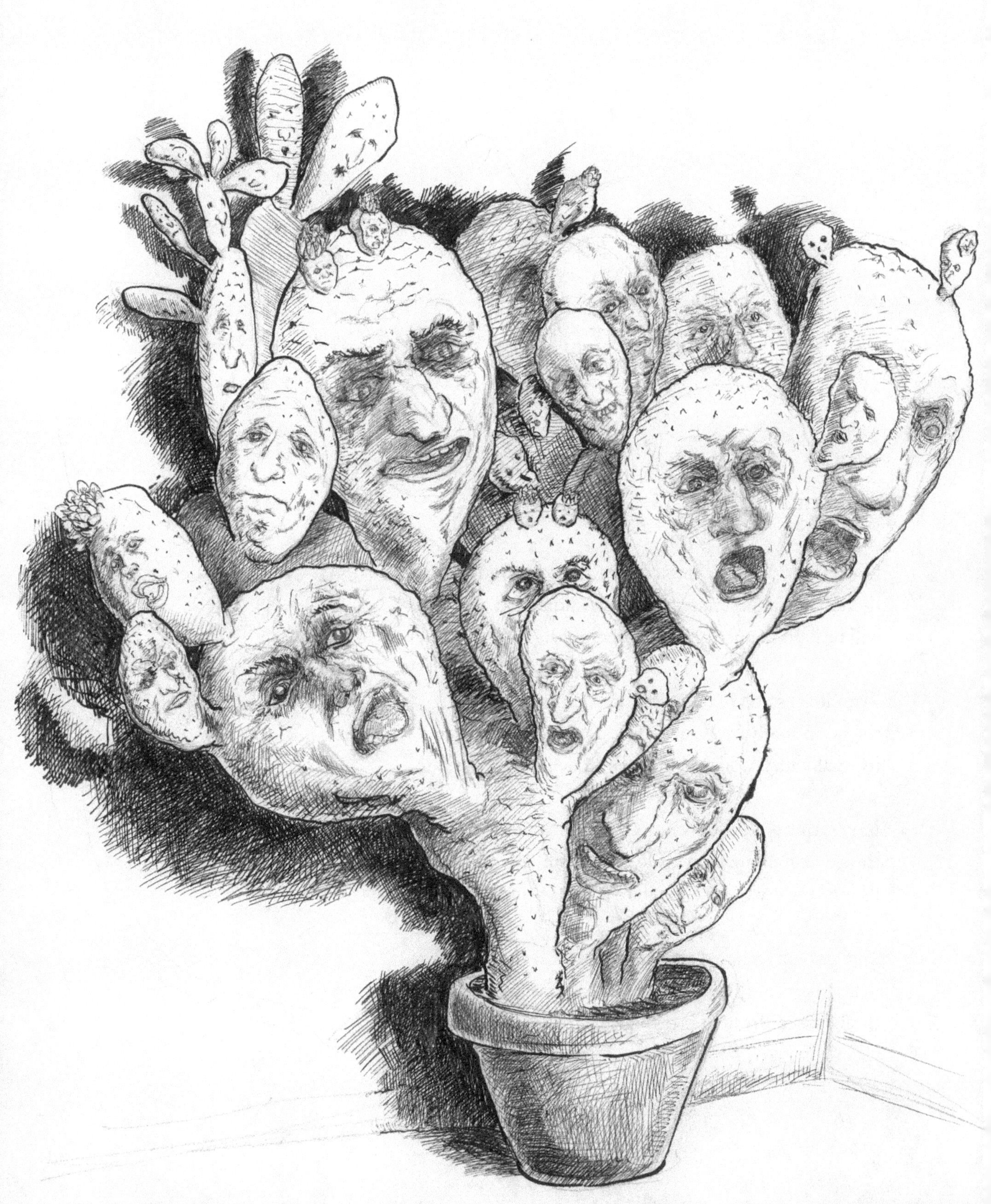

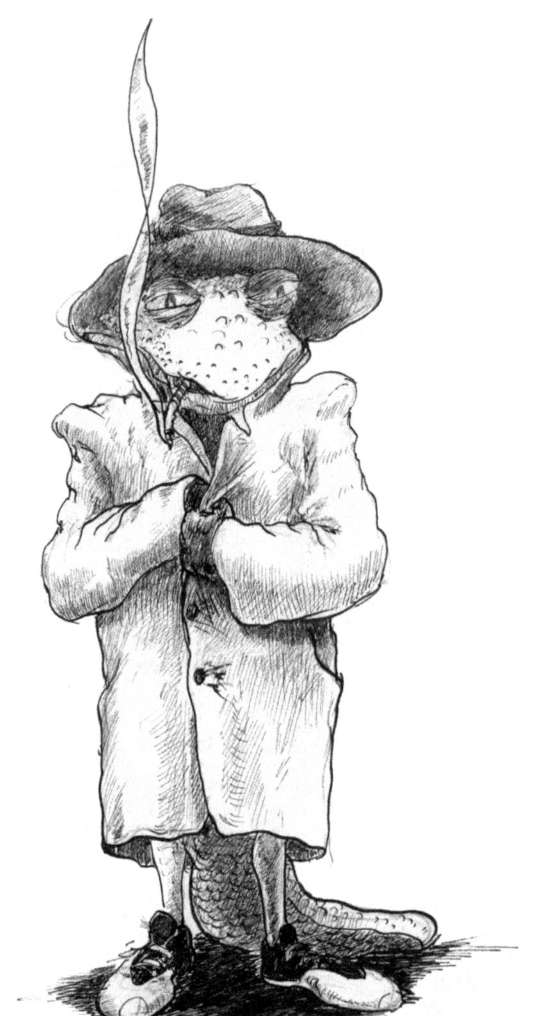

The Snide

Not as sneaky as the Snark or deadly as the Snub,
this antisocial pest, infesting every clique and club,
will lurk on the perimeter, fixated on the hub.

Twitchily attentive to the slightest innuendo,
the poop at any party and a face against the window,
its small talk is a silence that's approaching a crescendo.

Its greeting is a cul-de-sac; its strychnine wit is arch.
Its friendships are prehensile, and its smile is rich in starch:
its hunting cry is dry enough to cause a pond to parch.

The Snide, a spineless predator related to the Sneer,
will stalk its prey from either side, but pounces from the rear,
though if confronted face to face, it tends to disappear.

The Carrion Flamingo

— For Jeff Holt

The carrion flamingo is an undead parakeet
with ruffled feathers shades of earthworm pink, like rancid meat,
whose wingspread is high-handed, while its flapping seems effete;
its hooded glare is overcast with just a hint of sleet.

It lays an addled egg, abandoned just before it hatches.
Its heart looks like a casket or a book of soggy matches.
Its leprous skin is pale and pocked with sores; it sheds in patches.
The smirking beak invites you, though you wonder what the catch is.

Some lair in mausoleums, others underneath a rock.
Their voices shake like rattlesnakes. Men quail to hear them talk
about the corpses over which their sunset shadows flock,
and few sights are as ghastly as their limping, gimpy walk.

They stand as still as statues just before the chase is on,
and make folks blanch on mornings when they see them on the lawn,
carnivorous as hearses with the silken curtains drawn,
their plastic hues a mockery of rosy-fingered dawn—

then with a sudden muffled flap, they'll perch upon your sill,
to peek inside your window though you think they never will,
and feast those evil eyes upon you till they've had their fill,
an early dinner date with Death for which you'll pay the bill.

The Imaginary Friend

He had a little dog for eating schoolwork done at home:
as furtive and subversive as a mole that swims the loam,
dishonest as the day was long and honeyed as the comb,
he'd outlaugh your hyenas and was crafty as a gnome.

He wore the cat's pajamas, and he wore them inside out.
He yawned at ancient llamas while he rented room for doubt.
His smile was your umbrella. When you went on walkabout
and the way was straight and narrow, he would find another route.

An antic, antsy prankster heard to sing among the mimes,
he'd swing with Quasimodo, wreaking havoc with the chimes.
When he punished Dostoyevsky for some novel writing crimes
you took the blame, and had to write your name a hundred times.

The first to break from prison when Pandora took a peek
inside a box of chocolates that would last a child a week,
he helped drown all your sorrows until everything went Greek;
but don't believe your shadow died—he's playing hide-and-seek.

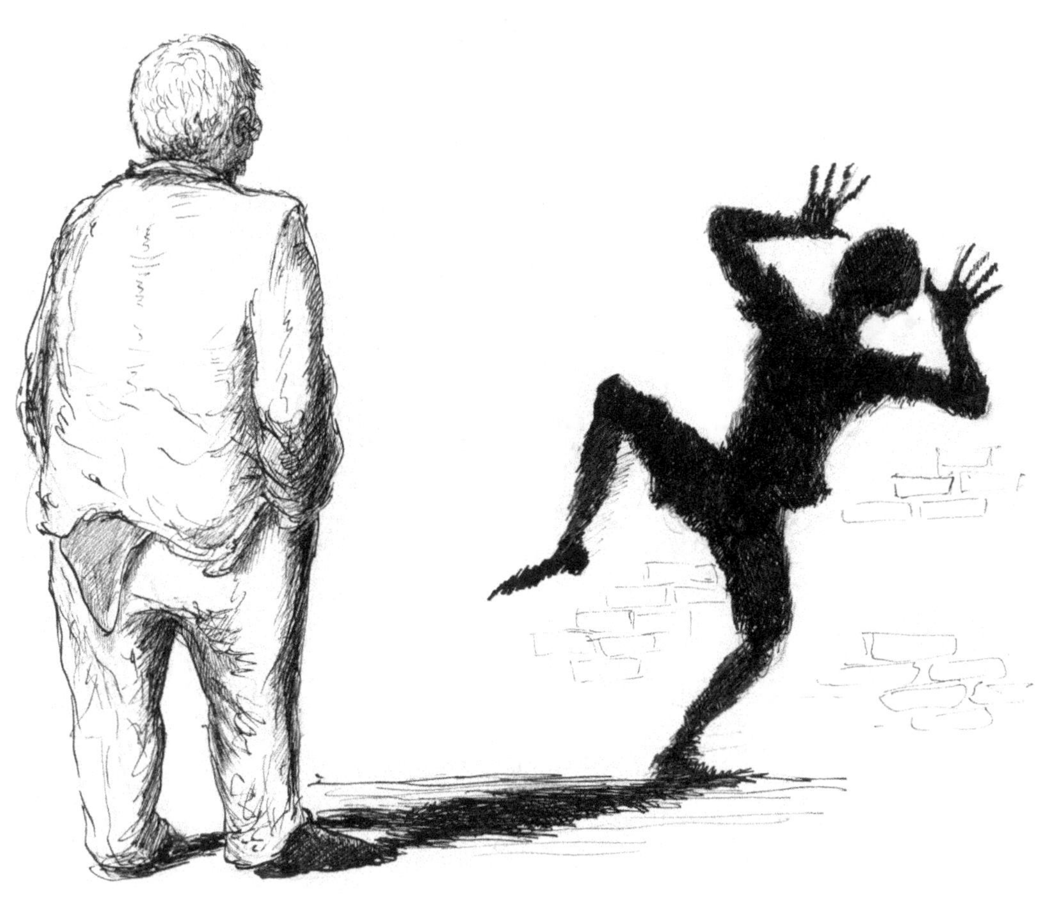

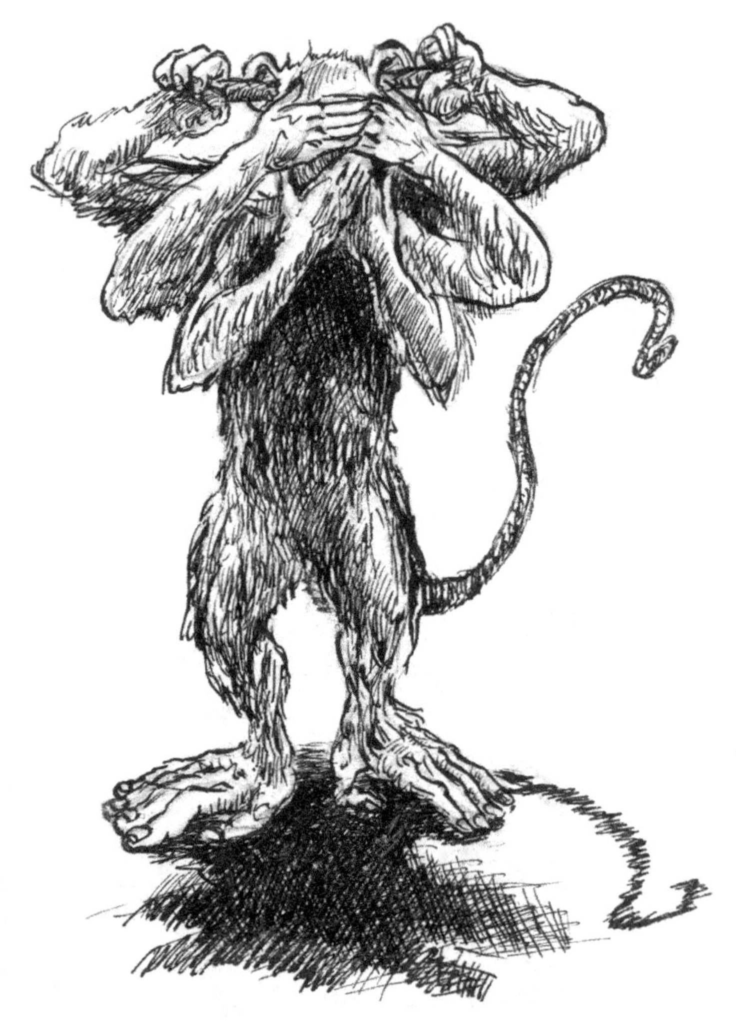

Making a Monkey

Monkeys see and do like men.
They love to ape our ways, but then,
even more the monkeys savor
how often men return the favor.

I Am What I Am

I am the money that talks in the bank,
a flaw in the mirror, a check that was blank,
the tip of an iceberg, the liner that sank.

I'm the isle of the blessed and the pirate who'd plunder it,
the veil of the night and the lightning to sunder it,
the boy in the bed and the monster who's under it.

I'm the sum of a part and the karmic subtraction,
the paralyzed thought and the frenzy of action,
the bile in my throat and a low satisfaction.

I'm the past I have checkered, the devil's detail,
the promise of love and a check in the mail,
rebellion in heaven, the quest for the grail;

I'm the grave of my death and the air in my head,
the puzzle I question, the answer I dread—
each shadow I've thrown, and the life that I've led,
the monster below and the boy in the bed.

Memoirs of the Widow Mantis

The man was an insect, a beast.
Devil-may-care and the color of kelp,
driven by instincts that no one could help,
he displayed no concern in the least
if our date was fiasco or feast,
and arrived, debonair, pre-deceased;
an eager groom who hastened to his wedding
like John the Baptist off to his beheading.

The heroine here, not the villainess,
I endured all his pre-coital silliness.
He had sex on the brain, not romance:
if I starved, would the kids have a chance?
He'd love me and leave me, the old song and dance.
It was fate. So I purred, "Prey, advance."

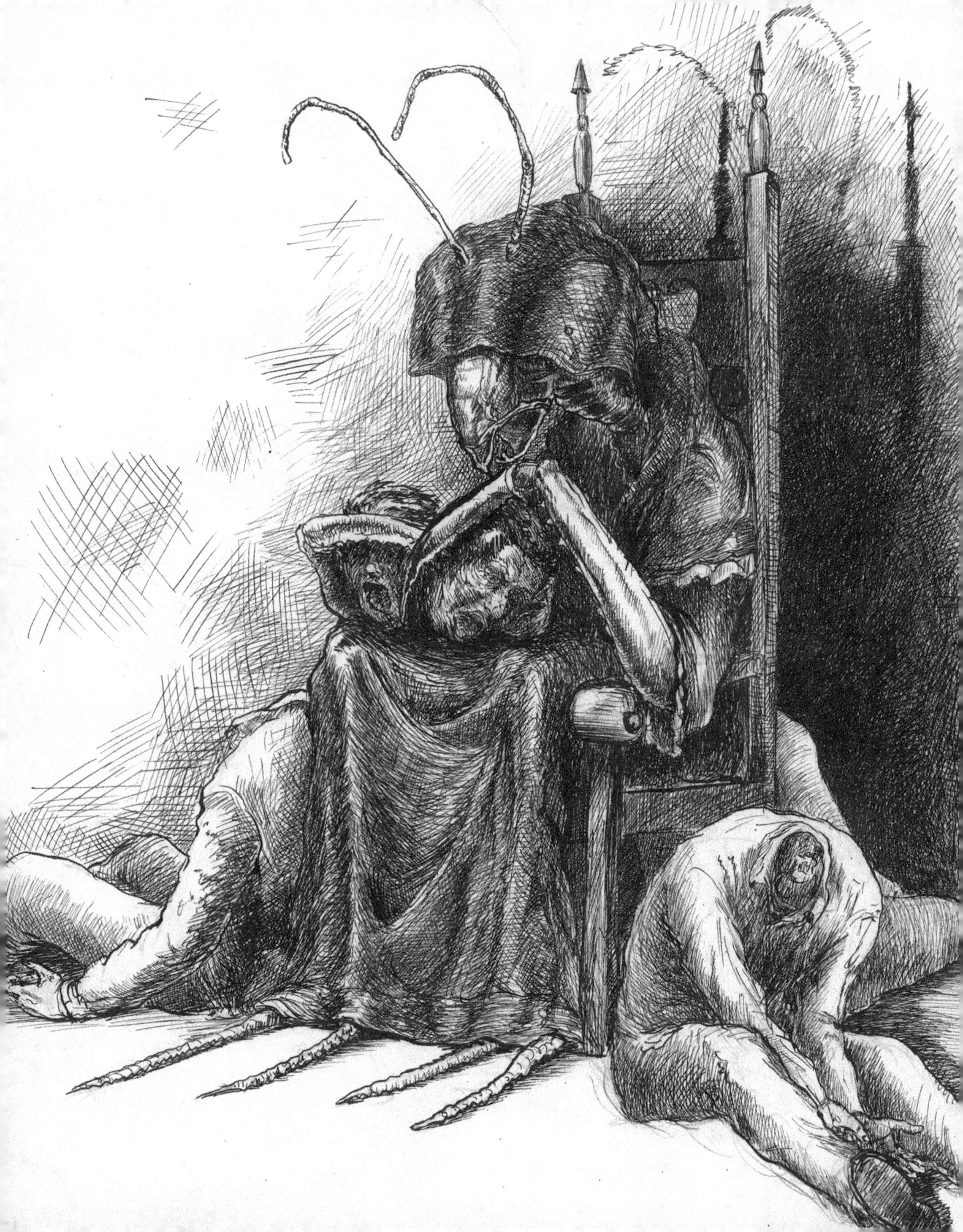

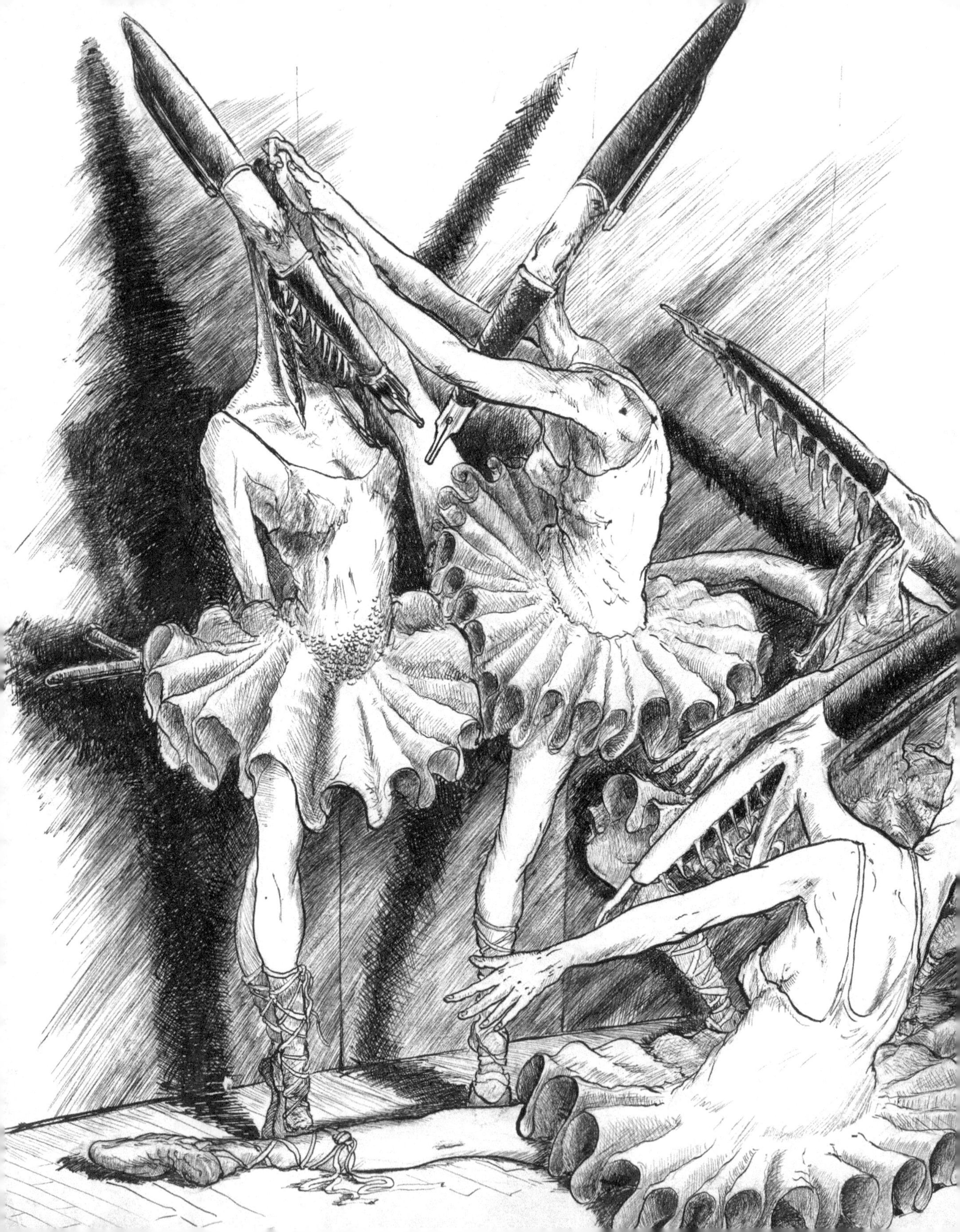

A Riposte of Gibes

The chilly edge of fashion, they wear pointed leather boots.
Instilling paranoia with their catty, haughty hoots,
they grill anemic Hipsters and make monkeys of the Snoots.

Thin as whips, their snapping turtle wits reflect their genus—
their eyes are funhouse mirrors, and their smiles flytraps from Venus
that turn inflated self-regard into a flaccid penis.

Their loyalty's so nimble one's imagination staggers,
and as they gyre and gimble Gibes have surreptitious swaggers.
Their morals are symbolic and their tongues are poison daggers.

They stare at utter bastards as they slyly mark the trump,
and parrot secret masters just to prod the toads to jump.
Take care, and don't be crass—reduce your ego, if it's plump;

beware these mock assassins, else your neck will be a stump.
Don't carry grudges massive as the dromedary's hump,
blare a barbed sarcasm at a slugger in a slump,

or scare the pants off fashion if you're actually a frump.
Don't glare from blinkered glasses; don't be heard to boast, or grump.
Be wary, gentle asses, or the Gibes will roast your rump.

The Stalking Horse

At first his chatter merely made you weary,
but he's persisted until now you fear he
isn't only odd but rather eerie;

especially when he moved onto your block.
Machinations masquerade as talk.
The nag it seemed he was begins to stalk;

and he will be your shadow day and night,
a clingy spider web that holds you tight,
the bit between your teeth that hides a bite.

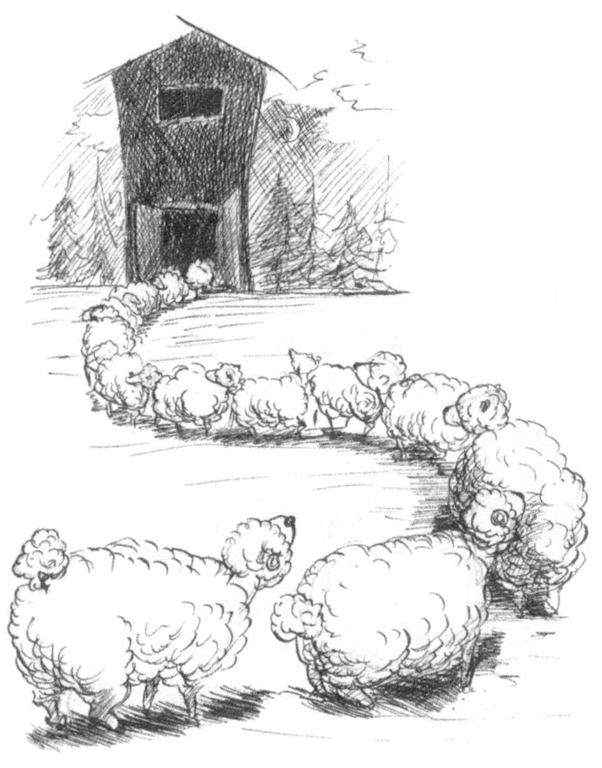

Sheep Is the Past Tense of Wolf

Their teeth are white, their lies are white, their laughs are bluff and hearty.
The halest fellows ever met, the life of every party,
they're well endowed, their ties are loud, their tailored pants are smarty;

yet heady drinks disguise their dregs—once golden locks start graying
and growing scarce as golden eggs they'd thought their goose was laying,
the chickens loosed in youth will come to roost and want repaying,

for there's more blue than yonder. When the bulls are cowed by steering,
and pigs begin to ponder why the aproned men are nearing,
smarter sheep may wonder why we stand in line for shearing.

The Otter

Otters are epitomes of cheer,
except the otters living around here.
Unlike the dogged beaver building dams,
the average otter's happier than clams
and outmaneuvers trout as if clairvoyant:
he's unafraid of depth because he's buoyant.

The otters around here, instead, are dour.
The fire in their eyes is damped; they glower
at those who pass them by the corner brook,
act like they've read or written every book,
avoid the sun, disdain the water's drench
while smoking cigarettes both thin and French,

and only swim around in dry vermouth.
What happened to the otters of my youth?

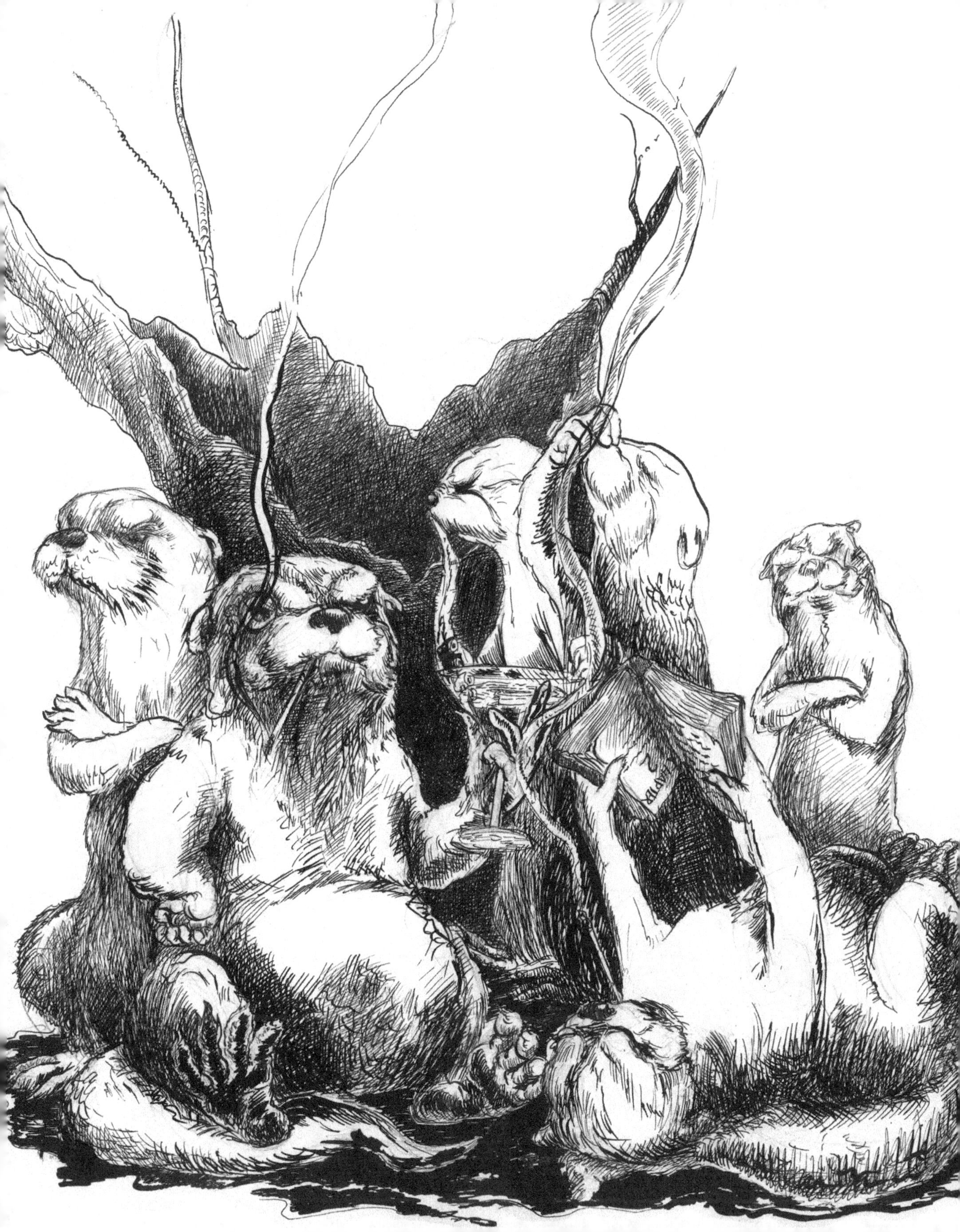

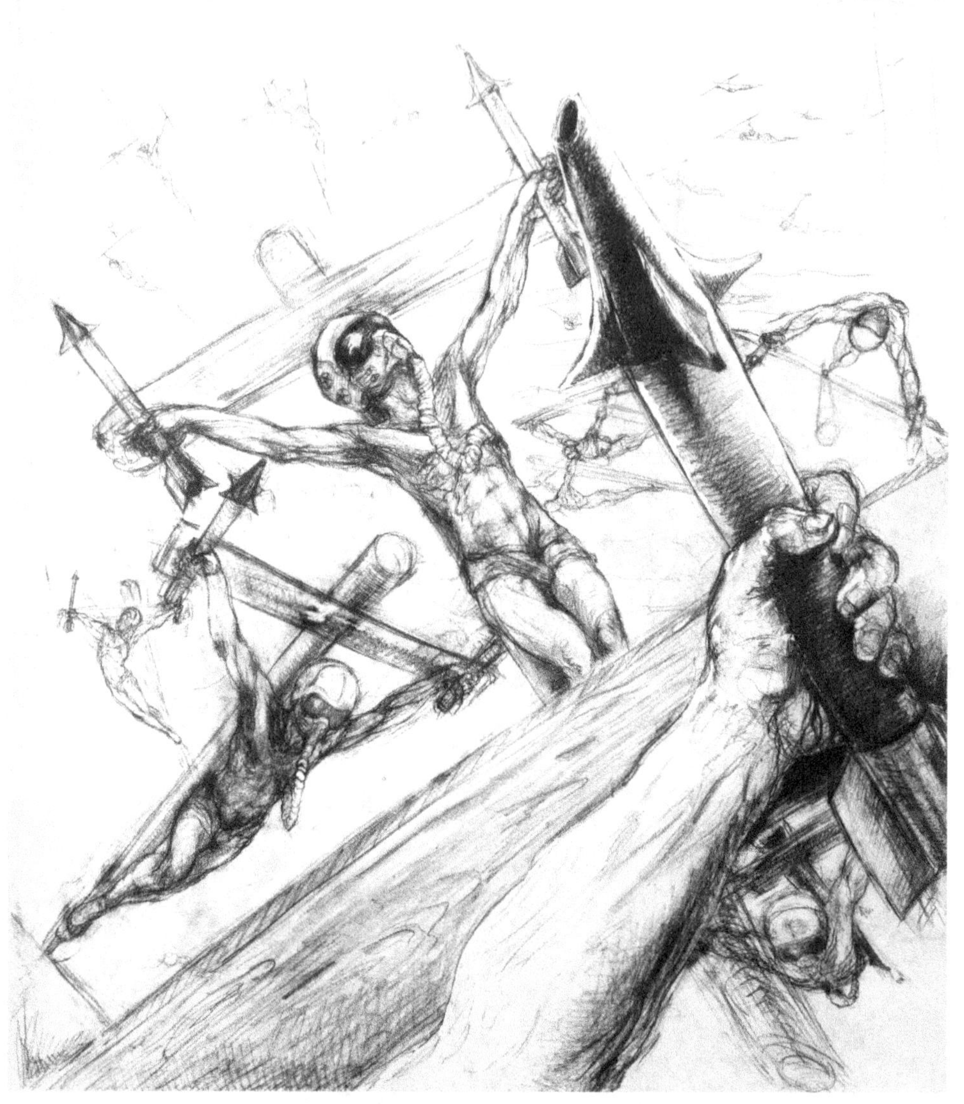

Butterfly Collection

Christ, immortal butterfly,
pinned and always on display,
bless this house, so prim and right,
where nobody believes in flight.

The Gift Horse

The gift horse is here
    with golden presents—
a crowd of well-wishers, lunging,
giddily jostle cargo meant
to salve the inmost longing,

for the one horse has come
    you will never find
and never will know a tether.
Desire becomes a whirlwind
that shakes its mane of feathers

as the gift horse arrives
    with Pandora's box
and St. John's head on a platter.
Medusa, in a writhe of snakes,
awaits the chosen rider.

The horned horse will rest
    in the virgin's lap,
the nightmare till night is idle,
the rocking horse, it will never stop,
though you clutch its cobweb bridle;

but the one horse everyone
    says they love
though they blanch at its bony face,
is fated to give all one wants to have
to horrified, avid applause,

till the gift horse, with its
    hidden teeth
and scaly skin of the serpent,
steals away quick as your darling's breath
on echoing hooves of argent.

The Pleasant

It couldn't be more pleasant, for it is the thing itself;
its visage blank, unlined, as pale as porcelain from Delft,
its mouth is full of goodness while its mind's an empty shelf,

and it's the very thing to be, unless it's not to be—
for should they march the neighbors off and lynch them from a tree,
the double-jointed Pleasant will bend backwards to agree.

A thing that's mostly nothing in its pleasant sort of way,
it's blithe as market bubbles. It's as malleable as clay,
its easy streets untroubled, for its thoughts police the day.

The days grow long and pleasant when the Pleasants rule the land.
The earth is flat, all paths are straight—they ask, but won't demand,
why their unpleasant children run, or die by their own hand.

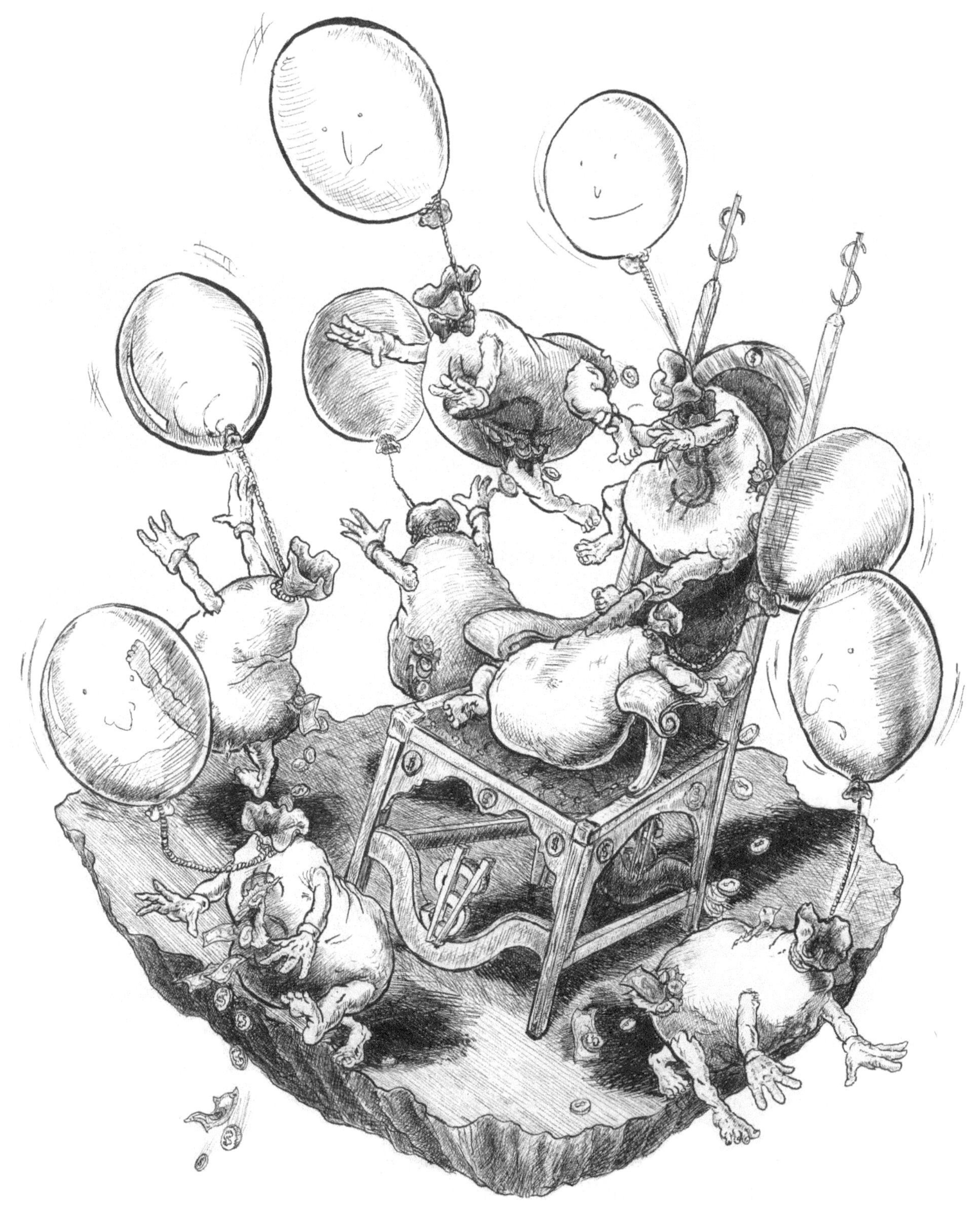

The Moaning of Life

When he was young, the sweetest nothings whispered in his ear—
the ace of Hearts was up his sleeve, the magic mirror clear,
and fortune was his darling till his twenty-second year;

but rising three-and-twenty, with the bloom still on the rose
that winked from his lapel, he heard a low noise, very close,
as if some new, unpleasant scent was tickling his nose.

It wasn't like a wolfish howl, nor like the serpent's hiss,
nor like that pregnant whoosh of Cupid's arrows when they miss,
for he had heard a moan or two, but never one like this;

something like the mindless sorrow of a midnight train
or what escapes from lips before the leap in lover's lane—
a tinny, mordant counterpoint that echoed in his brain.

He heard it, then, in pauses interspersing barroom chatter
in upscale dives where hogs got slaughtered while the pigs grew fatter,
yet when he tried to pin it down he found his wits would scatter

before a foolish answer mulish ears received as true.
But was it ancient wisdom that some ancient linguist knew?
Did it have a color? If so, was that color blue?

He tracked it with a Ouija board, but every shade declined,
and lost its thread of logic in the mazes of his mind,
a Disney castle Escher, Freud, and Kafka had designed.

He muddled on through shallow books as callow poets bickered,
and sought it like a fairy light within a swamp—it flickered
as the eternal Footman held his tattered coat, and snickered.

In the weeds, uncertain where the scruffy ball had bounced,
the match was called for rain, the final score left unannounced:
as he wept and wondered who had won and who was trounced,

the secret teased him with a flirty glimpse, then off it flounced;
and Cheshire cats kept smiling down at him before they pounced,
for life seems full of moaning if the meaning's mispronounced.

The Melodious Sappho

Her heart is big as all outdoors, and can't be blamed for that,
for love's her life, and she's as many lives as any cat.
She'll stiffen up your spine and such while loosing your cravat.

She'll open up your mind, and such is her infectious chatter,
you'll pitch her woo right back and she will strike out every batter
and leave you glad to be alive and madder than a hatter.

She'll leave you sad one day but with no doubt you will remember
how like the sudden flame that fills each leaf in drear November
she held a lump of coal, your heart, and blew upon the ember.

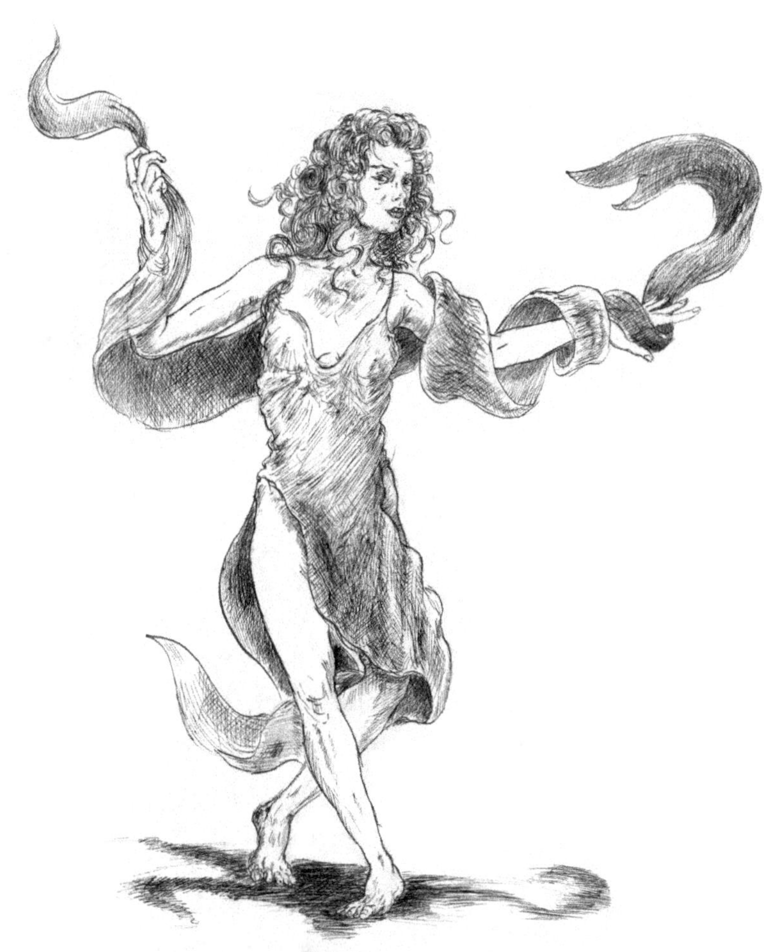

Monkey Manqué

My suit is not my birthday suit.
I chew cigars, eschewing fruit.
My wild is dreamed, my jungles, roomed.
My tribe is one. I'm never groomed.

My paradise was lost, then walled,
whatever Darwin started, stalled.
I use my thumbs to thumb my nose.
I walk upright—it's just a pose.

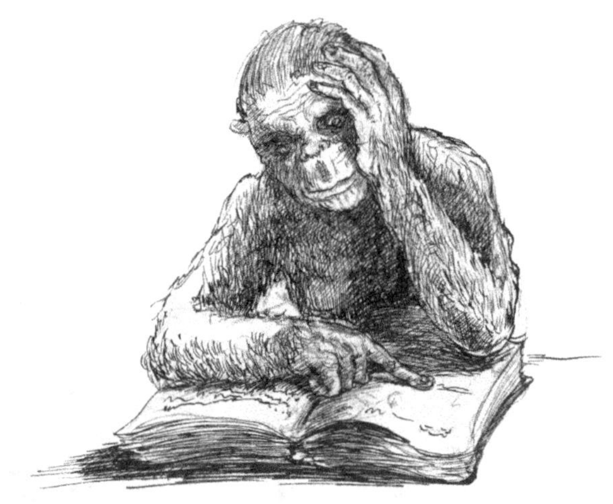

Darwin's Monkey

Ancestral imp, not yet evolved
enough to mark our riddle solved,
why leave the foliage for the folly
and ape your master's melancholy,
or grow unwise enough to look
for all the answers in a book?

The Gilded Void

A monkey with a dash of shark, its airs are often aped;
its soul has heavy curtains, and it keeps its conscience draped.
Its thoughts are closely guarded but its feelings have escaped.

Its hide, gilt-edged, is scaly, while its blood is palely blue.
It laughs, but never gaily: as it grins, it gives a view
of teeth like small stilettos plus a kitchen knife or two.

Its lamprey tongue's a burglar; its veins are berged with ice.
Its posture's posed, and poised. It postulates the poor are nice,
and couldn't love them more than when it's carving off a slice.

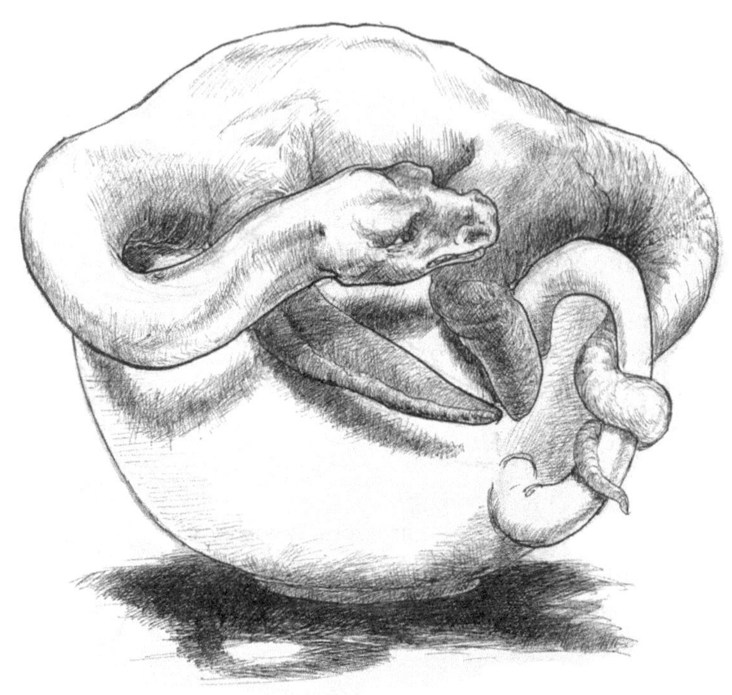

Loch Ness

I’ve never lived near lochs like Ness—
the lakes I like are stocked with less.
Their fens are penned. The glens are gleaned.
The geese are cooked; the fishes, cleaned.

Such lakes, bereft of boats and docks,
their size approved by Goldilocks,
are somewhat dry; their waves are ordered,
the grass close-cropped, the beaches bordered.

The sneak that snakes about in lochs,
though fierce and furtive as a fox,
is fortunate I stay indoors,
for monsters aren’t a match for bores.

The Terrible Beauty

A terrible beauty is born.
—W.B. Yeats

The doctor and all of the nurses
went in shock, then erupted in curses
as he held the odd babe up with scorn
when the Terrible Beauty was born.

Nine planets will wither, like plants,
all the canticles shrink into can'ts,
and the stars will be starlets of porn,
for a Terrible Beauty is born;

and the mirrors will empty, then splinter,
the breath of spring turn into winter
and cows will get into the corn.
When the Terrible Beauty was born,

the bang and the whimper threw dice—
no one knows if it's fire or ice,
but the angel is lifting his horn:
a Terrible Beauty is born.

Now the dead have lurched out of their tombs
as room for doubt runs out of rooms,
and there's no one alive we can warn
a Terrible Beauty is born;

and the Heart of the Dark is aflutter,
since the changes are stark, even utter,
but the death of the night is the morn.
A Terrible Beauty is born.

The Wyvern

A kind of dragon without arms, these flying snakes with legs
are blind and weak as kittens when they crack their speckled eggs;
but first the tail grows long and barbed, and then the back grows spikes,
and once it's grown to fifty feet it eats out where it likes.

Once it's twice that size, a wyvern's bigger than its britches.
It steals the neighbors' silverware, their jewelry, coins, and riches,
but never spends a penny though it grows as rich as Croesus,
and won't give an allowance to its nephews or its nieces,

who once were weak as kittens, too, but grew up nursing grudges:
they skulk around the wyvern's lair, to see if uncle budges,
and then attack with flaming breath or monstrous halitosis,
for wyverns will not share a thing except their shared psychosis,

and gladly kill or die themselves to keep the loot they've plundered—
that's why they're scarce as honest men, in case you ever wondered.
But if you see a pretty kitten, blind and very weak,
the forelegs sprouting downy wings, with scales upon its cheek,

you could set out warm cream, then tuck it in with *Puss in Boots,*
or buff it till it gleams as it outgrows its birthday suits;
or teach it French and Latin, plus the proper way to sit,
or buy a satin hat for it to wear, if one would fit.

You could pretend it's friendly, like a puppy, although bigger,
and when it's playing cat and mouse, refuse to pull the trigger,
but soon you'll be a mouse yourself, and that's a sticky wicket.
Imply you're going out for smokes, then buy your one-way ticket:

for there are many states, estates, or states of mind, at least,
where no one's even heard of such an avaricious beast,
where everyone is kind as cows, the tragic end's unwritten,
and friends will lend a burlap bag to drown the likely kitten.

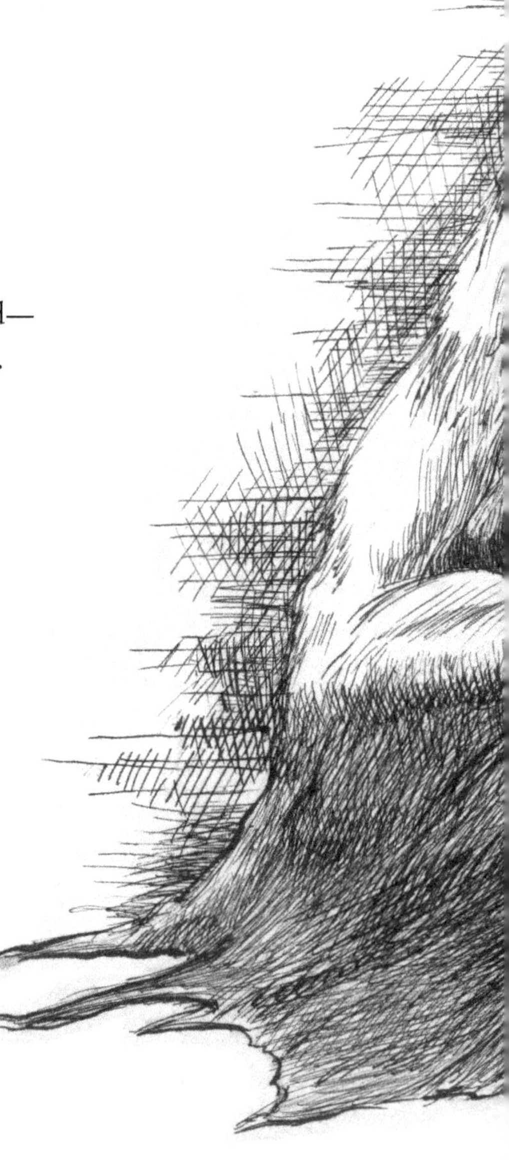

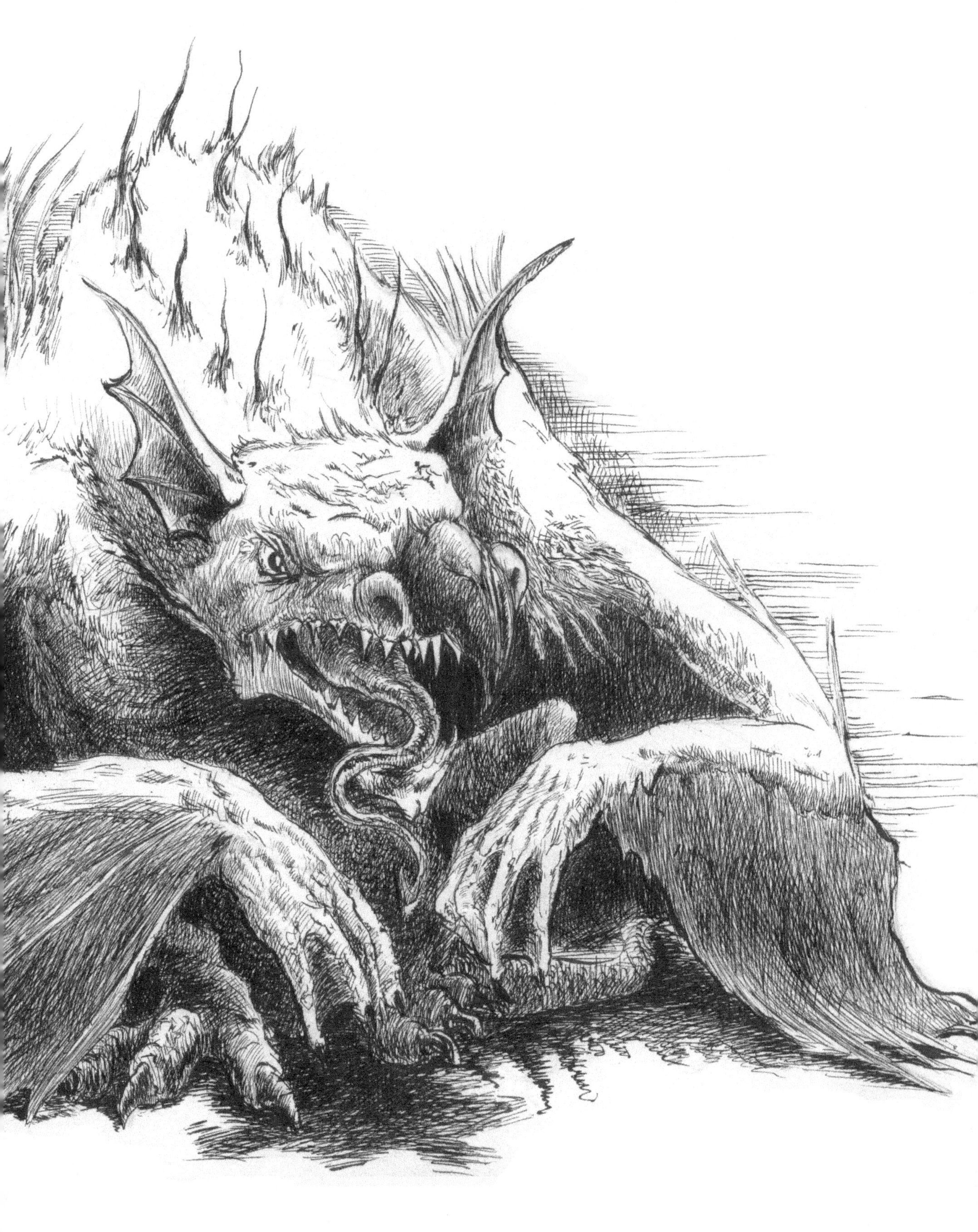

The Dog-Eared Mystery

Like a teasing Christmas box that comes too tightly wrapped
or *terra incognita* filled with errors once it's mapped,
the mind is like a leopard that the lion tamer's trapped,

while hearts resemble leopard spots that try but never change,
darkly shifting camouflage for keeping prey in range,
bargains with the devil lovers make in fair exchange;

and God's an engineer: the local runs slow
through valleys folk may fear and alleys you'll take pains to know,
but when the ticket bought so dear gets punched, it's off you go—

for life's a dog-eared mystery, though each one ends the same,
engrossing till the plot goes missing by the final frame,
the book without a butler where it looks like we're to blame.

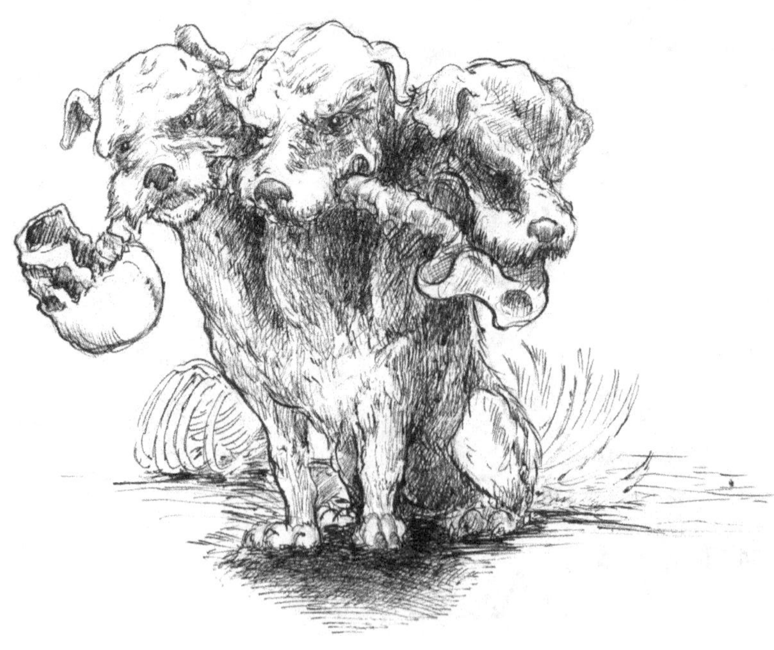

The Flowering of Noon

He wished he knew the mind of God, and wasn't odd—like you,
he wished he had a tongue of flame, knew secret names, to woo
colossal, cross-eyed sheep and an apostle, maybe two.

How they'd marvel as he warbled like a serenading whale
in a shower built of marble, watered by the holy grail,
with virgins riding sturgeons round his feet to hear the tale.

In ivory towers of his dreams he'd gaze, with eyes of moon,
and make the evil cower as they felt his sharp lampoon,
then retire to his bower, till the flowering of noon;

and kings would dance attendance like a ring of circus bears.
He'd declare his independence, he'd divorce himself from cares.
His soul, in swift ascendance, would provoke the angels' stares.

He'd take his tea with Buddha, break unleavened bread with Jesus,
then astride a barracuda he would sample fragrant cheeses.
In the warm and fuzzy mood a man has sleeping when he pleases,

he'd dream until the Trumps of Doom and never close his eyes,
and astigmatic grumps who had assumed he was unwise
would look up, glumly stumped, and see a heaven full of pies.

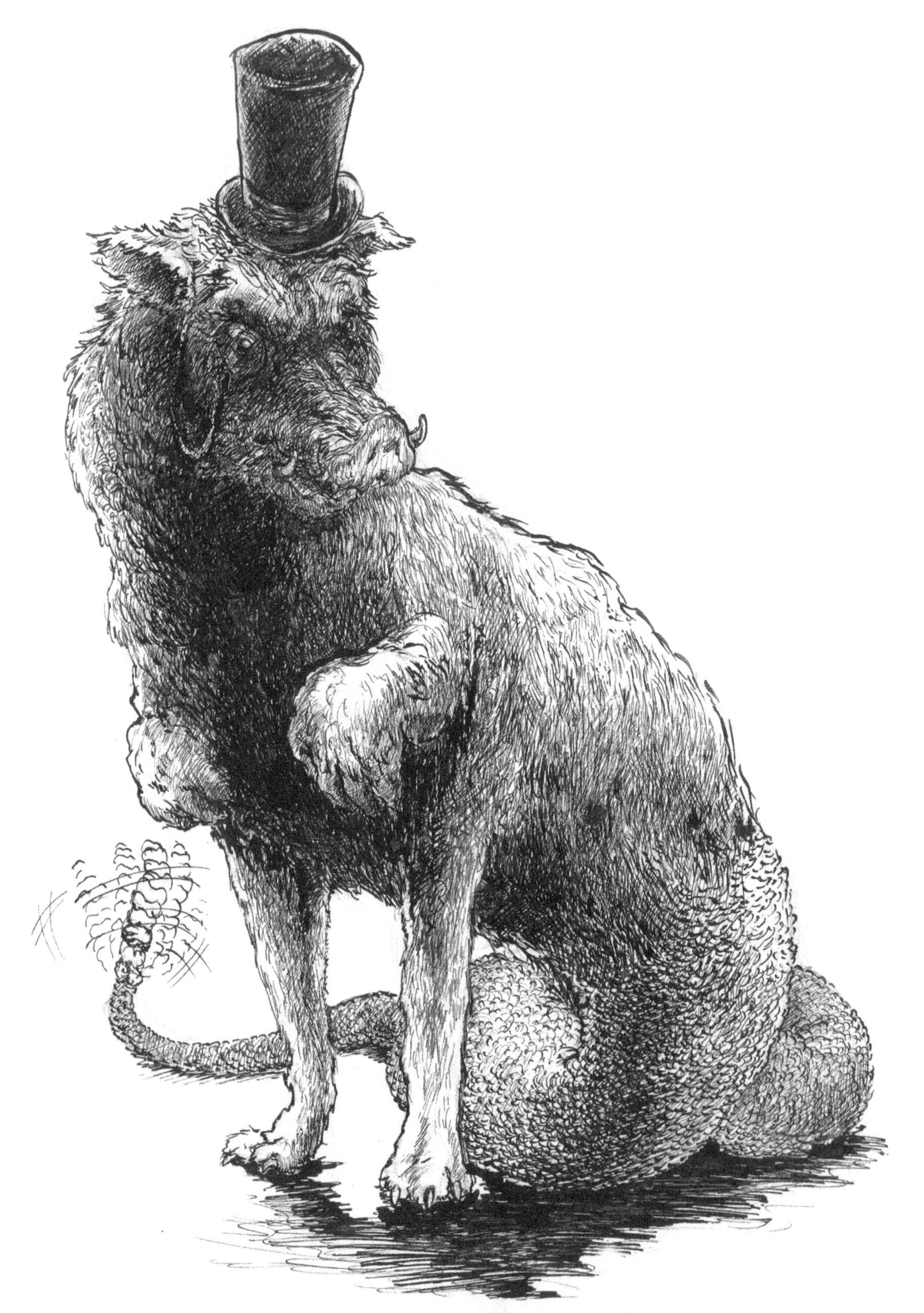

The Slink

Charming as a flophouse with a bathtub full of adders,
it flouts the laws of science, slickly climbing social ladders
by trickling antisocial thoughts like urinary bladders.

Its tongue's a snaky shadow. A disruptive syncopation
of moves behind the scenes forecasts its leapfrog ambulation.
Its hunting cry a subtle, slimy, sly insinuation,

it's scoped us out as birds to pluck, but first it plans to fatten us
on patter slathered lavishly with compliments gelatinous
and up to seven deadly sins to tempt the inner brat in us;

yet larger Egos love a Slink, and never feel alarm
till one has stabbed them in the back while walking arm in arm,
selling Brooklyn bridges while it's buying them the farm.

The Common Retronaut

Its native gait a stately one step forward, two steps back,
this crusty slug—too fat to fly, yet sure it has the knack—
is drawn to ivory towers with the windows painted black.

Its Doppler hoot is thunderous. It feeds a fretful Brood.
Its self-regard is ponderous. Its retrospection skewed,
its future is foreshadowed and predicted by its mood.

It glides down straight and narrow paths amenable to bending:
flattered by dawn's early light, blindsided by the ending
where pesky karmic debts are rubber stamped *Past Due* or *Pending,*

its air is philanthropic, yet it pinches every penny.
Its morals are myopic; as to hope, it hasn't any.
Its Latin name means *Legion:* even one can seem too many.

Great White Hunters

The evening you confront the fabled yeti,
your knees will knock; your hands will shake, grow sweaty
and wish that pocket knife was a machete:

for camouflaging snow falls like confetti—
your friend who shoots and misses will regret he
bragged he'd spread its pelt upon a settee,

as if within a still life by Rossetti;
and when it slurps your innards like spaghetti,
I'll clap, then burp the yeti.
Is that petty?

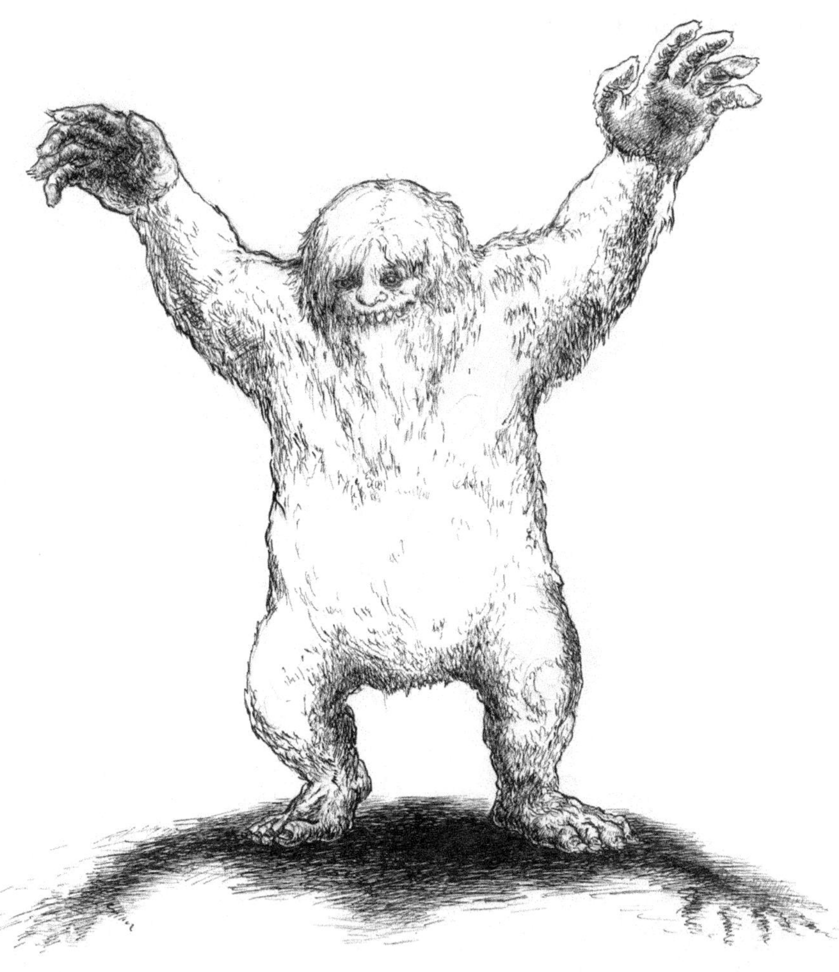

A Pry of Gossips

Their mating call a whisper with a culminating snigger,
their ears are large as pitchers but their mouths are even bigger;
their gums are flapped unflappably with great panache and vigor.

Resembling a gecko with a raspy double tongue,
a quick, distorting echo with a bellows for each lung,
they hang on every word and leave us wishing they were hung.

They buzz about the carcass of an ass, which is their hive,
make garbage their repast and haunt the graveyards, where they dive
for juicy buried bits their rancid breath will bring alive.

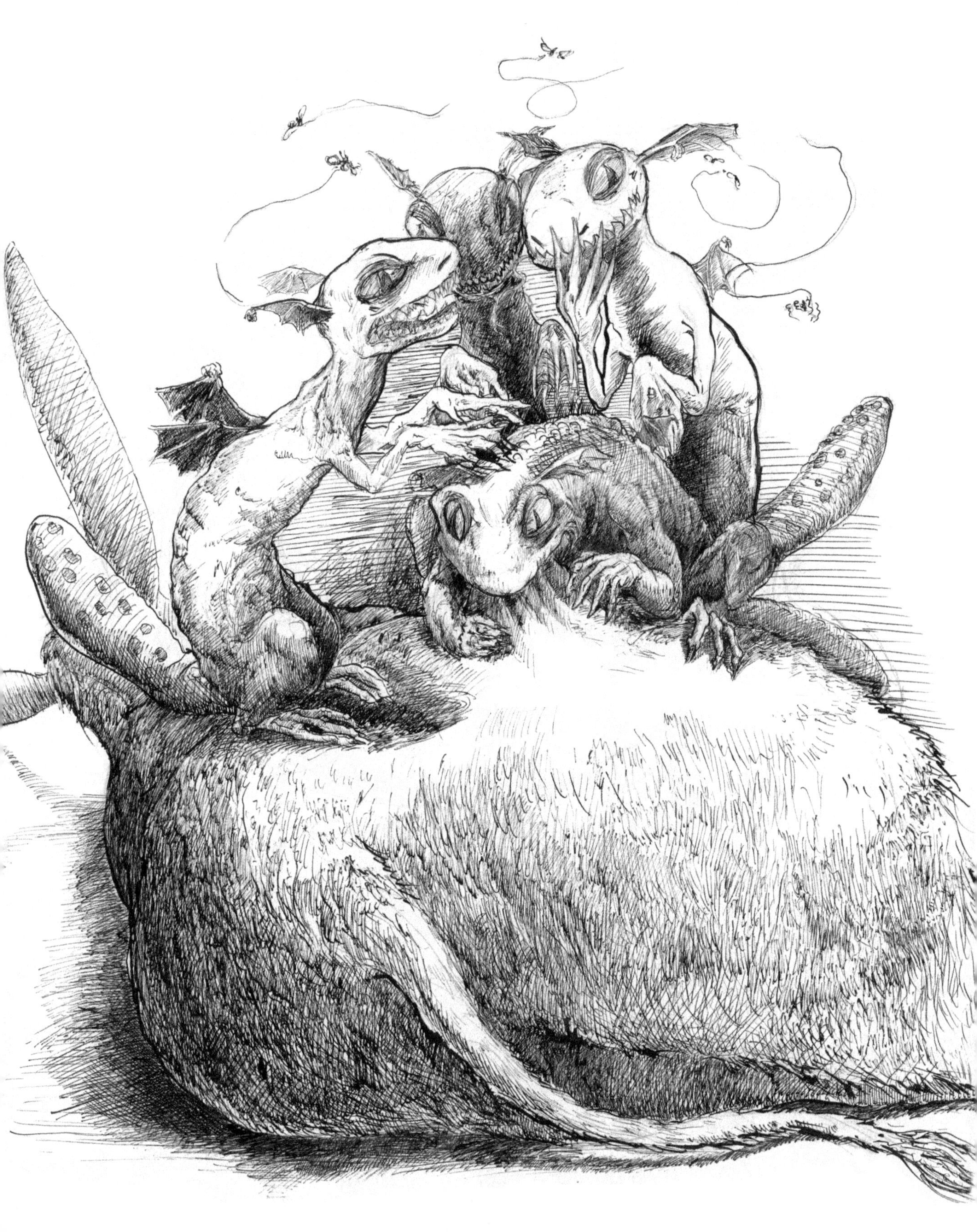

The Ravenous Dream

I starved the dream, till it was light
enough for me to carry,
and though its ribs were sticking out,
I nursed my daytime worries.

I stuffed it in a pocket, snug
if smothered in my wallet;
wingless now, an eyeless grub,
I don't know what to call it

now that it's small enough to scream,
a nightmare growing from a dream.

The Camelopard

A clawed, carnivorous canard,
the lethal, lithe camelopard
is partly leopard, partly camel,
mostly myth and maybe mammal.

It dines with djinns on drifting dunes
beneath romantic desert moons,
and seizes sheiks, who shriek like mice.
A cat with humps, a plot device

dismissed by those who know the rare
is equal to what isn't there,
it's half mirage; yet few still doubt
who view its spots from inside out.

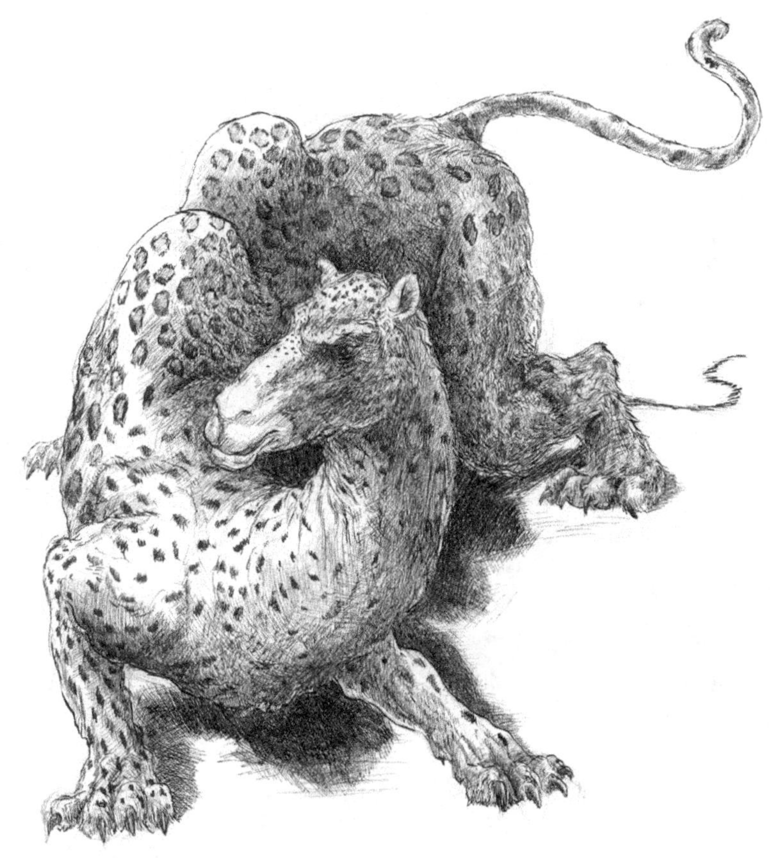

The Camel

I sometimes fancy I'd look very
stylish on a dromedary,
but camels can't imagine seeing
themselves beneath a human being.

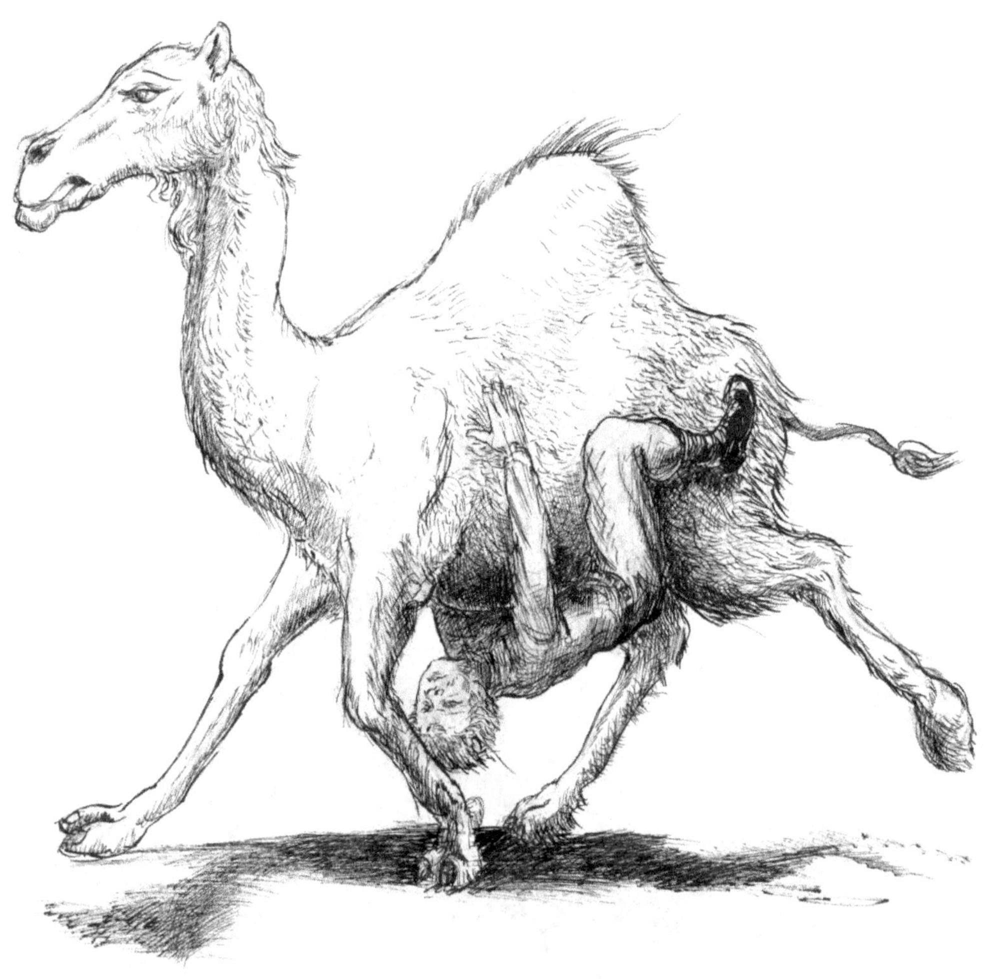

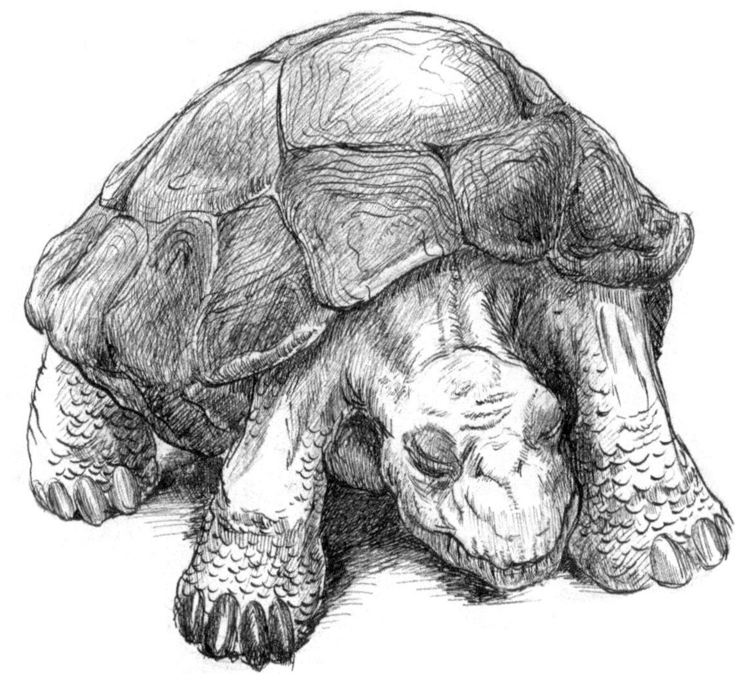

The Tortoise

The tortoise is the swiftest beast.
He proves the last is not the least.
His view is long. His legs have shutters.
He loiters in his house, and putters,

dislikes the dash, prefers to snooze,
would be a stone if he could choose;
an armor-plated, languid mole, he
embraces fleeting moments slowly.

If Wishes Were Horses

I wish there were an island flush with mangoes and papayas
and natives plumed in feathers like the atavistic Mayas,
who'd sing the runic epics as they tended evening fires.
I wish there were an island on the sea;

and winds with piquant spices like the chili of El Paso
would blow upon the lively waves beyond the mild Sargasso
with latitudes of freedom, and a horse you couldn't lasso,
as fleet as any wind, would come to me;

and I would give her carrots, sugar cubes, and bits of apple,
and by her wordless kindness on a back of silver dapple
I'd ride without a saddle on a horse you couldn't grapple.
Oh, what I'd give for such a thing to be;

for like the wind we'd travel on the piquant island's beaches
and laugh when cynics caviled as we sought the outer reaches
beyond the judge's gavel and the politician's speeches,
as careless as a wind and fancy free.

We'd hide upon an island near a city made of granite,
just past the sooty towers on an overcrowded planet,
an isle that can't exist outside of childhood dreams—or can it,
if what we wished had waking eyes to see?

The Night Circus

Against the wall your hands become a hound,
and then a black giraffe with just a twist.
These chiaroscuro beasts cannot be bound,
yet twine while pairing perched upon each wrist.

Two questions posed and answered in the night
will solve the dark in moments when they tryst,
and meld together, redefined by light,
adumbral blossoms rising from a fist.

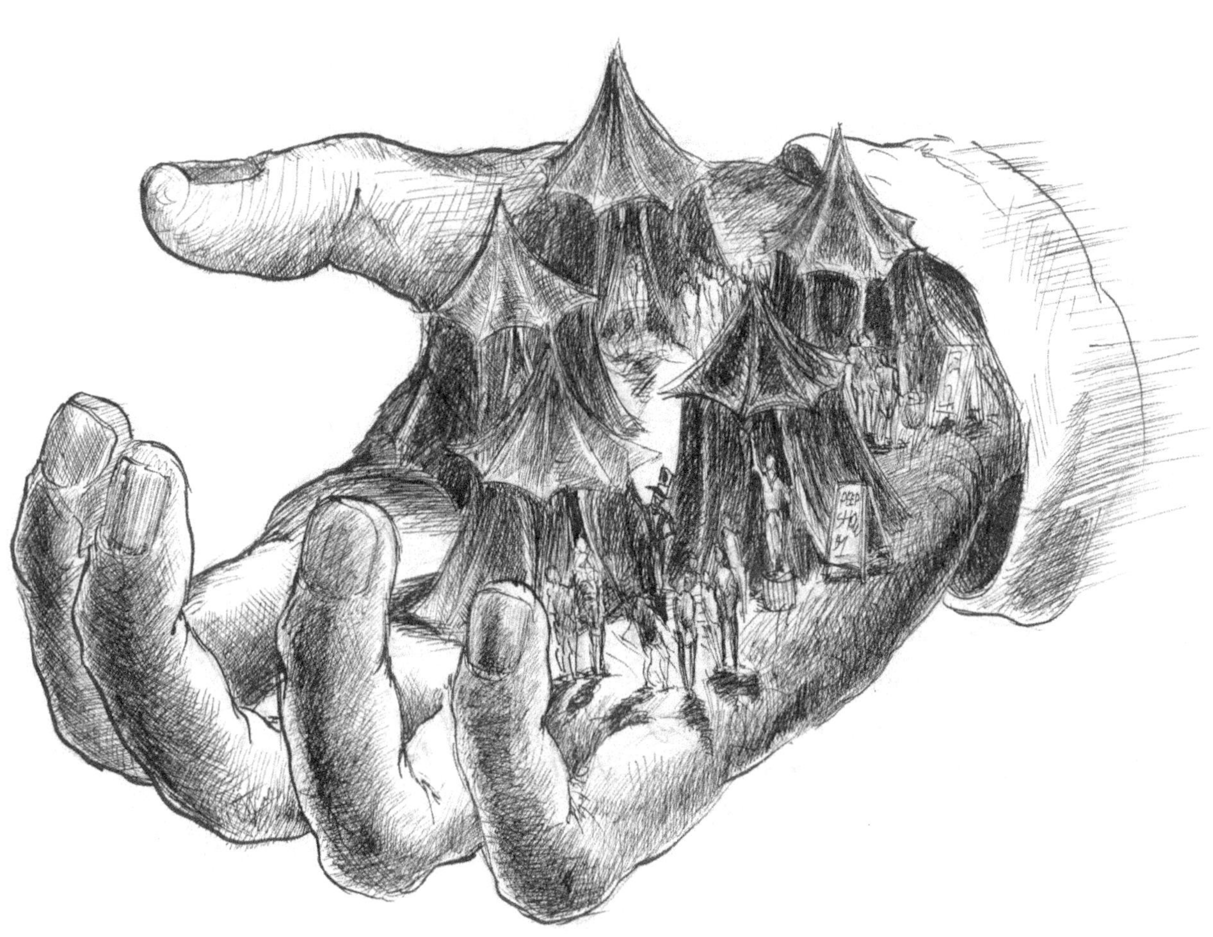

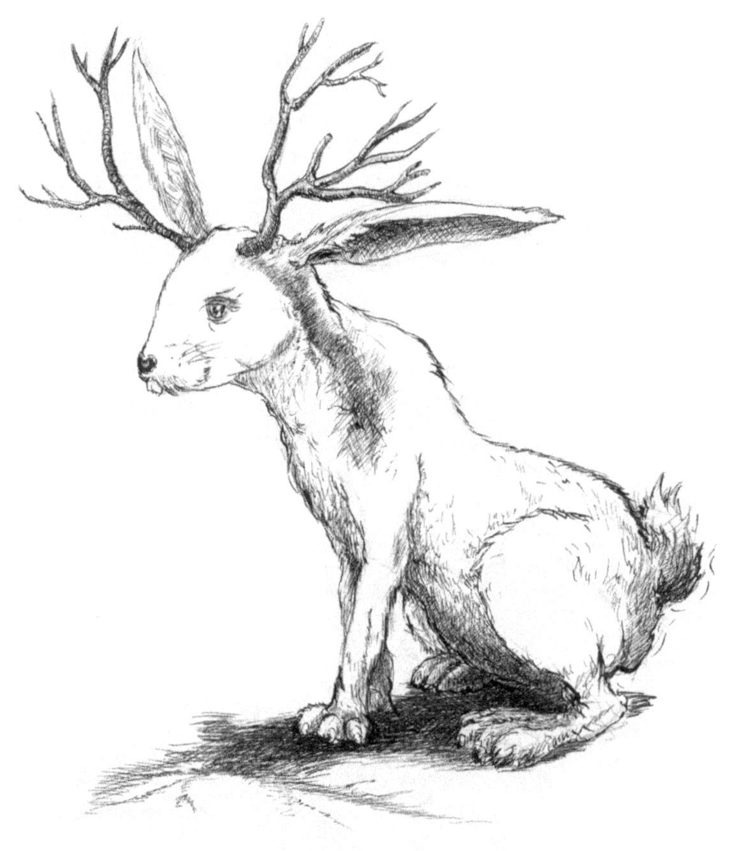

The Jackalope

Marvels of the taxidermist,
belief in jackalopes is firmest
in ivory towers, kindergartens, taverns,
crazy-as-a-coot prospectors' caverns
and states where hare and deer are commoner—
isn't that some strange phenomena?

A Zaftig of Hippos

Resembling a river-going barge,
the thinnest hippopotamus is large,
while larger hippopotami are vast
and won't be faster beasts until they fast.

Pandora

There weren't a million evils, only two,
for all I found within was me and you—
and just a glimpse at truth was all it took
to be condemned by those who wouldn't look.

Balloon Animal

Most are strung along by the tightfisted
or dream of flying free, but I insisted
a straight and narrow life should be resisted—
the party won't begin until you're twisted.

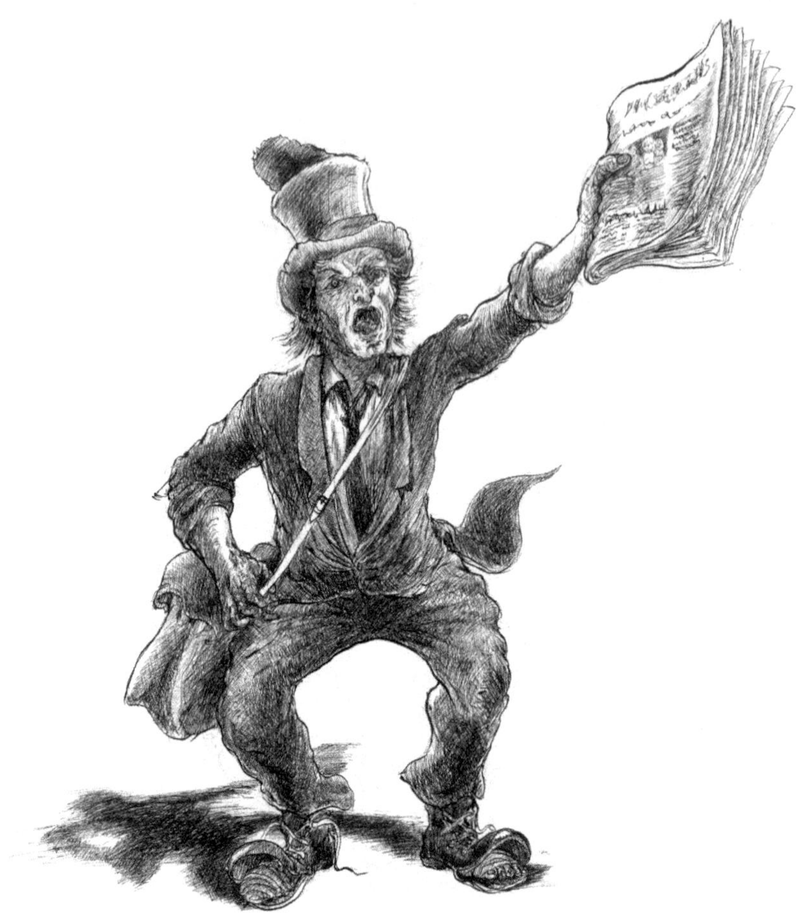

The Lesser Pundit

A pimp of pulp whose prophecies are evanescent puffing,
akin to spineless serpents due to skin he's prone to sloughing,
the Pundit's busy body's like a turkey filled with stuffing.

Producing pygmy insights while gigantically outspoken,
a tick whose verbal tricks suffice to fix what isn't broken,
his slot machine of wisdom can be played for just a token.

Defeat is in the orphanage, but wins have lots of daddies—
the Pundit is their uncle, and is famed for claiming that he's
always landing eagles but is snickered at by caddies.

The Golden Calf

Times were hard—the roiling crowd, unruly,
believing life's a television serial
whose laughter tracks embarrassed them unduly,
demanded prose both purple and imperial.

The promises the idol strung together
were catchy nonsense jingles if they'd listened.
Its hide, so thin, was stitched from shopworn leather;
a fool could see it wasn't gold, but glistened.

They longed for cul-de-sacs and picket fences,
with neighbors twice as white as Marley's ghost.
In hindsight, through the rosiest of lenses,
they caught a glimpse of what they wanted most,

and they were sold, for God was dead or missing—
a brazen moo would answer every prayer.
What did it matter what the snake was hissing?
The Trojan Horse was none of their affair.

The Dodos

Like flamingos run to fat and dimly dumb,
or commas on their sides, with little feet,
an awkward sign the end of times had come,
I watched as dodos doddered down our street:

or was it all a dream? They seemed to smile—
their smiles were fixed in place; they fit right in,
for cul-de-sacs are something like an isle,
the way a stubby wing is like a fin,

the way a television's like an eye,
or suburbs are like towns, or clocks like time,
or dodos are like angels waddling by,
or Liberty's the backside of a dime.

With no more thought than we they built their nests,
as dogs and cats prepared a proper greeting
for those who quailed at questioning, and quests,
and dully viewed their doom from comfy seating.

A Now of Hipsters

Careful, picky herbivores—at least while others look—
they mimic artful poses from a famous obscure book,
and cannot stand the kitchen's heat but snicker while you cook.

Their cigarettes are slim and French; their silhouettes are thin.
Their fads are trad; their shirts are plaid. They sip absinthe, not gin,
and should you find the place they flock they'd never let you in.

An object of their mirth, you're here on earth to let them gripe,
for Hipsters can outsnob the Snub, their snips eclipse the Snipe.
Never, ever intimate their name derives from *Hype*.

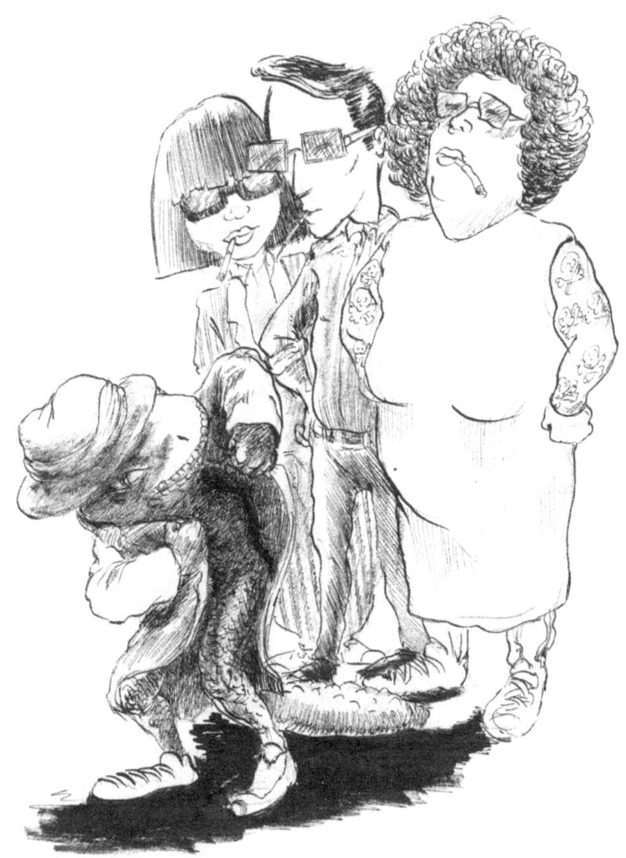

Let Down Your Hair

Like Goldilocks, I'm off in search
of the bed that feels just right,
not the soft, too accessible perch
where strangers commute at night,

nor the hard one, the bed of nails
with blankets so small and thin,
or quicksand, which conveniently fails
to explain what I'm sinking in,

but the bed, as the fairy tale goes,
that isn't too lumpy or brittle,
and doesn't cut off or stretch my toes
for being too long, or little.

I don't want a tortured affair
with some growly old bear that could bite;
Rapunzel, my dear: let down your hair,
wherever you sleep tonight.

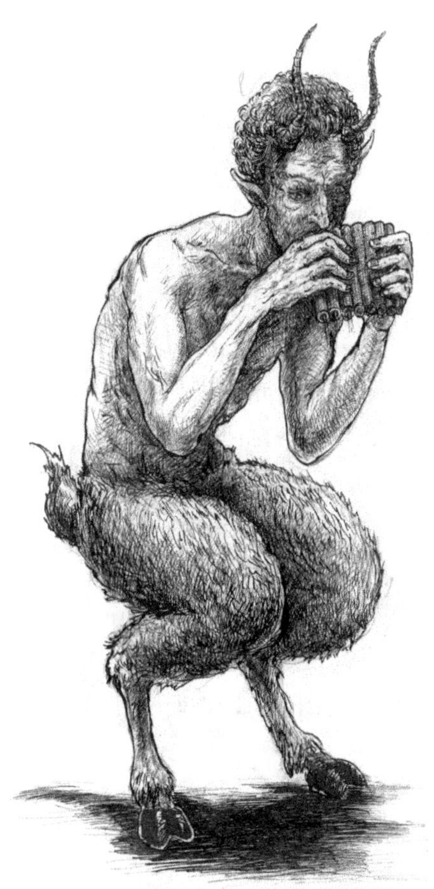

The Satyr

Priapism: (noun) a delusive state in which men make mountains out of molehills

He never sought out fame, but notoriety—
seduction, revelry, and insobriety,
a golden age for fools in Rome and Greece,
priapic wars against domestic peace.

It's said they got his goat, and Pan is dead,
but lovers often spot his tracks in bed
where man and goat and god are all the same,
though men give either gods or goats the blame.

Spider on a Pillow

You're not the first damn fool to dare the climb,
and maybe not the last to find this bed
a brief detour, or just a waste of time,
as instincts, blindly followed, are misled.

A few have been entangled here, and yet
you'll find the ties that bind can break or fray—
departed lovers prove this, so forget
complex, unwholesome plots to make them stay.

What self-delusive urge could make you spin
this web for catching pillows, wind, and dust?
I'd laugh, except the fix I find you in
resembles hopes I've cherished that went bust,

for what we seek is seldom what it seems.
So few find comfort in the land of dreams.

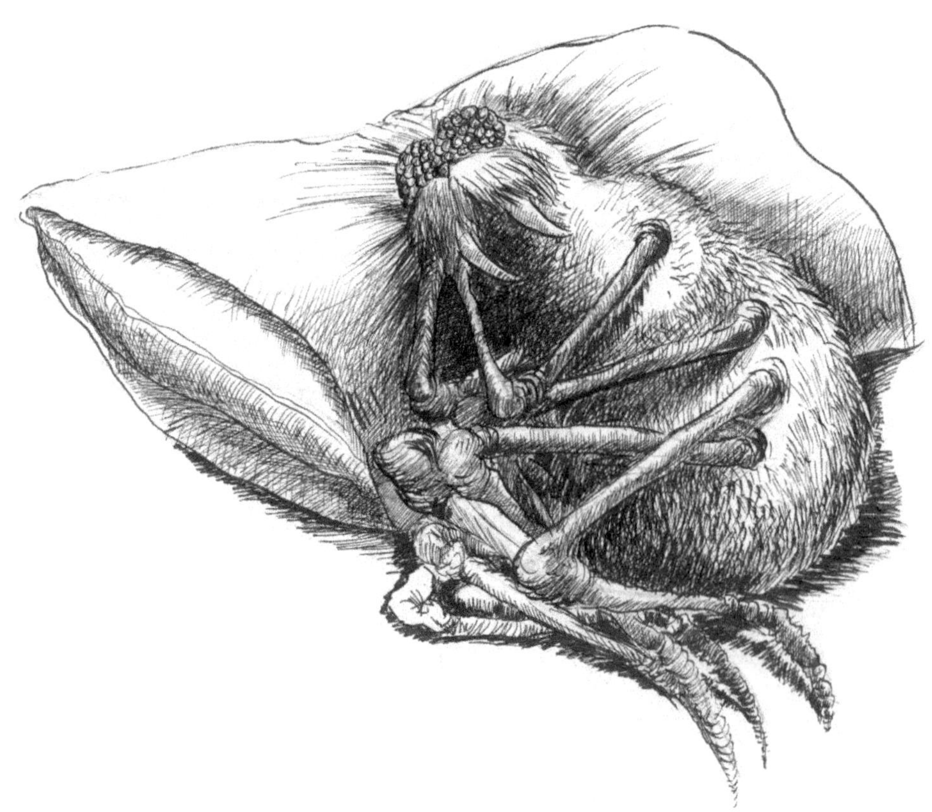

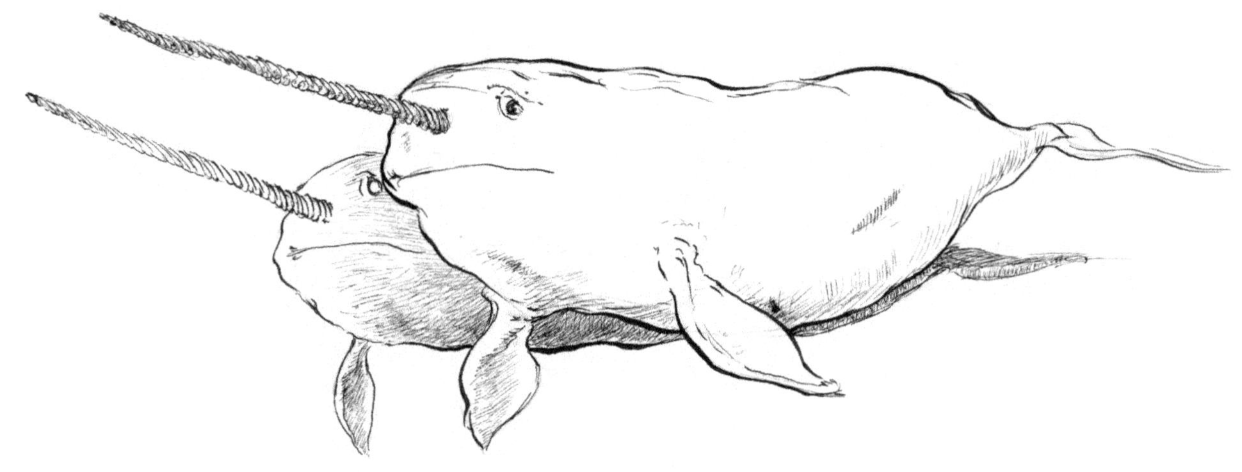

A Joust of Narwhals

Little longer than its horn,
part cigar, part unicorn,
the narwhal frolics, disinclined
to use a sword to speak its mind.

Men have always found it odd
peace should flourish in a pod,
flummoxed that these placid creatures
won't employ their martial features,

inciting fights on what their use is
amongst the apes on arctic cruises,
till decks are swarmed with skewered corpuses,
alarming the disarming porpoises.

The Doppelgänger

I try to sneak around him, but he always sees I'm there
and catches me on mornings when I'm vulnerable and bare.
Stepping from the shower, feeling springy as a rose,
about to shave—it's then the saggy, wrinkled horror shows;

and like a little bird I stare into his cobra eyes,
and like a sinner staring at his sin there's no surprise.
This glass of bitters, falsest front, whose kindred face is blind,
the wafer-thin façade above a shallow frame of mind;

a karmic shadow aping me, my tragicomic mask
who'll match me stride for stride, though I'm not equal to the task.
My mockery, my mime, my evil clown, my own poor skin
whose faults stand naked to be seen, except what lies within.

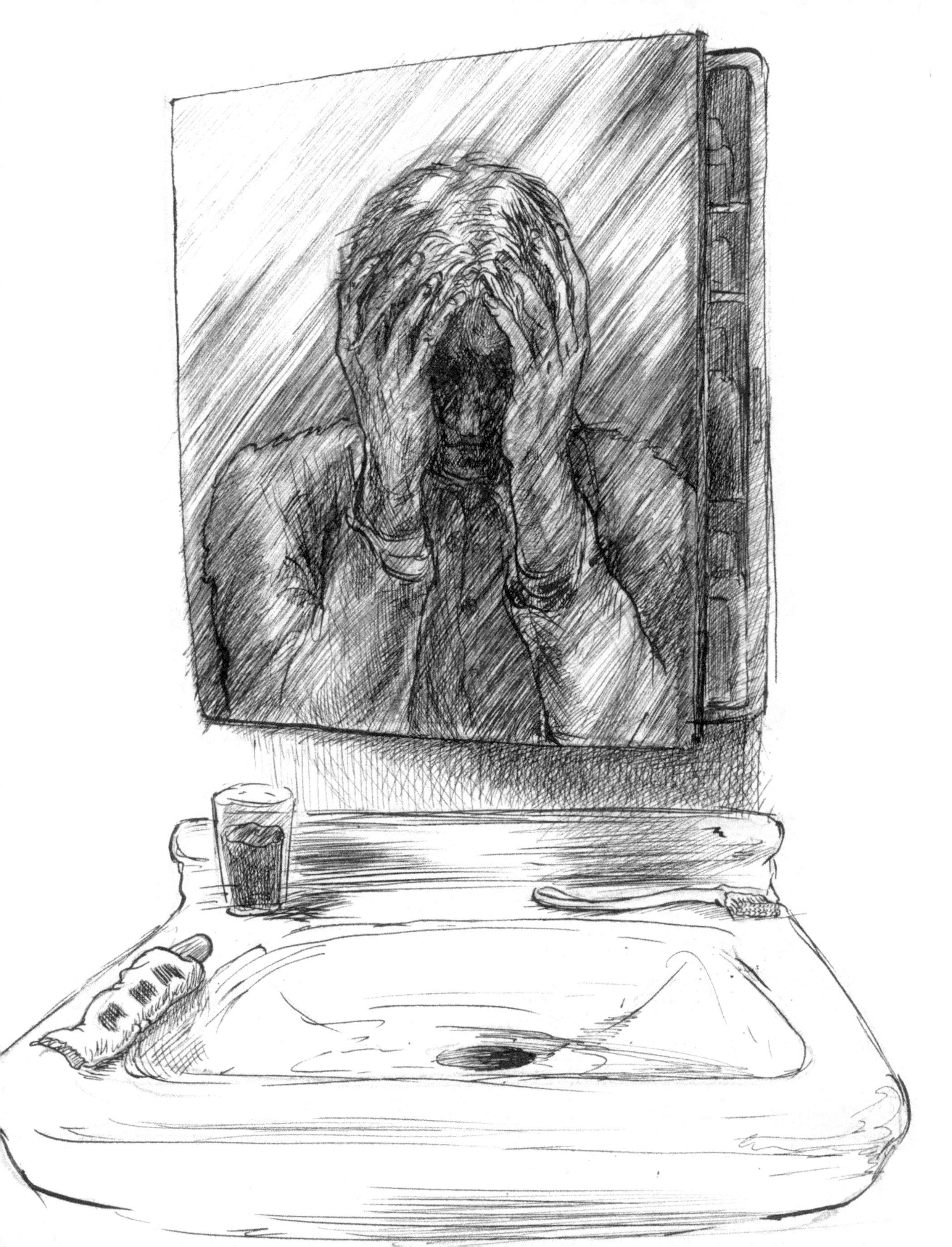

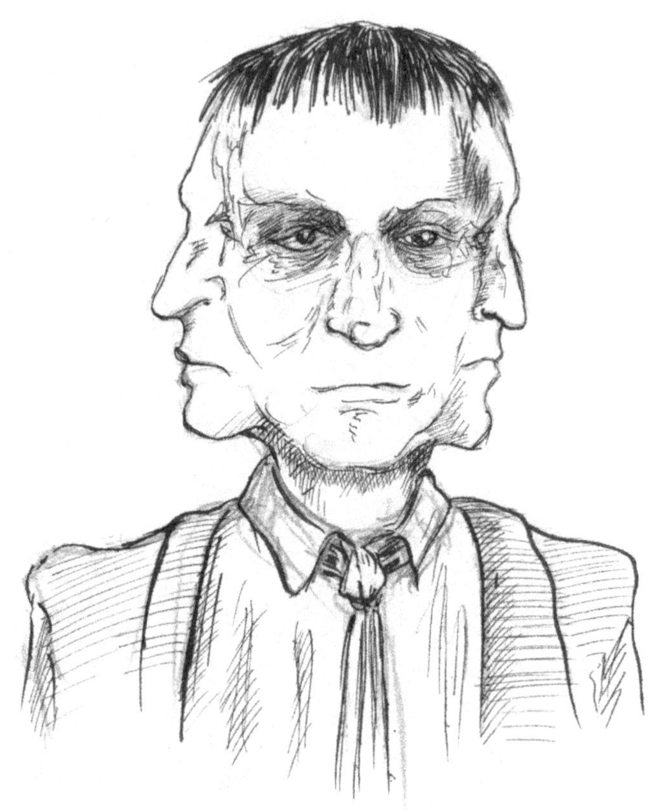

Pod People

You are you and I am you
and we are also you.
When you are I and we are here
all differences will disappear,

like words a mynah bird repeats
or houses on suburban streets,
redrawn by what the pod erases—
one person, wearing different faces.

The Beast in the Jungle

A hydra-headed rose, a crown of thorns about to bloom,
a smell that got inside your nose and tickles like perfume,
you sense it's close: a silver lining, hiding in the gloom—

or else an icy sliver sure to shiv you in the cold,
piranhas in the river you'll be crossing once you're old,
ties that bind but sever all you thought to have and hold;

a shadow bound to follow, though you've led a merry chase
around the inner hollow while you flee a dark embrace,
the beast you've feared will swallow you with its familiar face.

The Snipe

The Snipe is quicker than the Snub and fiercer than the Snide.
As cold as ice, its needle nose, mere millimeters wide,
slices slightly thicker wits and pricks balloons of pride.

A kind of Grump, beside itself when lovebirds start to pair,
it finds the Pleasant rather plump, the Hipster rather square,
reunions rather boring and rejoinders most unfair.

A scuttling nest of scorpions, its scheming brain is arid:
its blood's a seething acid, and without an ounce to spare it
has massacred more innocents than Vlad Dracul or Herod.

It snips at kinfolk, skewers foes: its valveless heart a vault,
it aims its pique at blameless backs, then claims it's all their fault.
Its young are nursed in Punic fields the Romans sowed with salt.

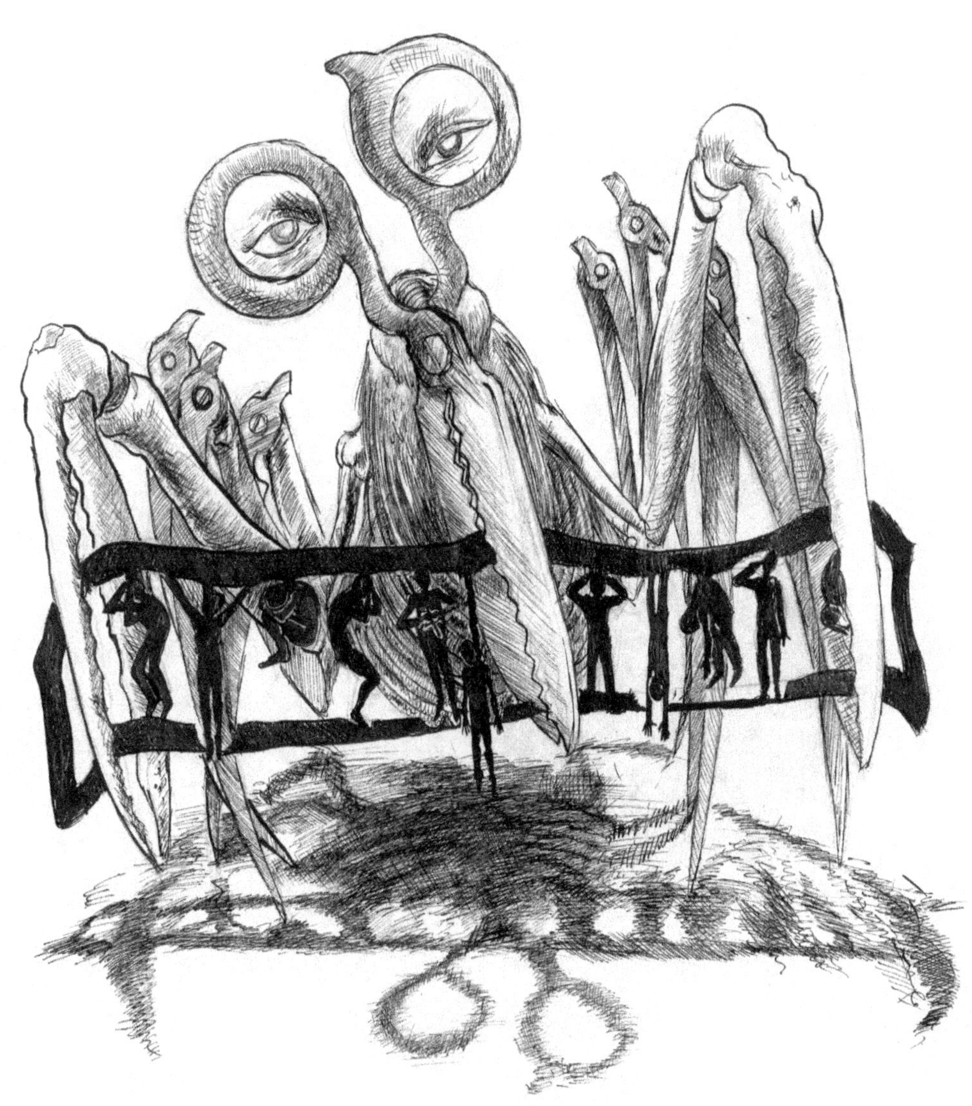

The Rabbit in the Hat

There is no rabbit there—
I've reached inside for years
and just come up with air:
but disregard your fears
and those whose wits are thick,
for reaching is the trick.

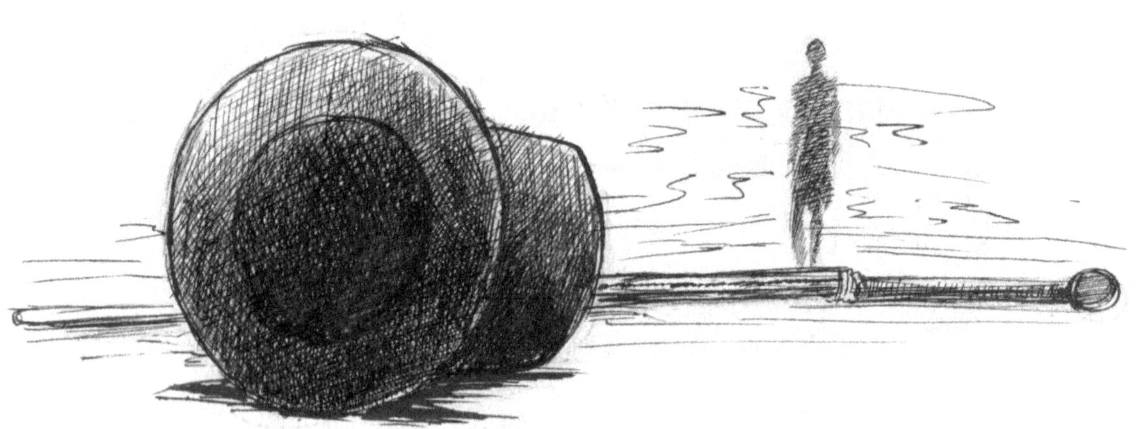

The Inkling

The Inkling is an infant thought, or else a dying vision.
Its rival breed, the Brood, seems blurred, and murmurs like a pigeon.
Some are groomed by Prufrocks until doomed to indecision,

some are drones, some worker bees in search of a position;
others grow entrenched and fight a war of slow attrition,
want everyone to cater to their delicate condition,

or bark without a bite because they lack the right dentition.
Most eat themselves, like starved ideas, balloon past recognition,
coil in knots, are boiled when caught, or spoil before fruition.

My own's a fancy coupe without a key to its ignition.
Designed to race, it's parked and locked, afraid to chance collision,
as tigers idle in the tank, too tame to budge a smidgeon.

The Prim

A squeamish beast, the first, the least, abstemious and slim,
its mortis has great rigor but its vigor has no vim.
It thinks it walks on water, but it won't learn how to swim.

Wincing at vulgarity, it minces into pews
where sermons fortify its soul with nicely sorted views.
Mortified if hemlines hint at life above the shoes,

it walks a straight and narrow line: its gait sedate and sure,
its thoughts, though small, are very fine. Flamboyantly demur,
its blush is rose. It holds its nose. Its mind, kept closed, is pure;

for Prims reside in shuttered rooms without a cozy seat,
uncluttered, trimmed in pale pastels, and lacking any heat—
Christian soldiers without peer who fear to cross the street.

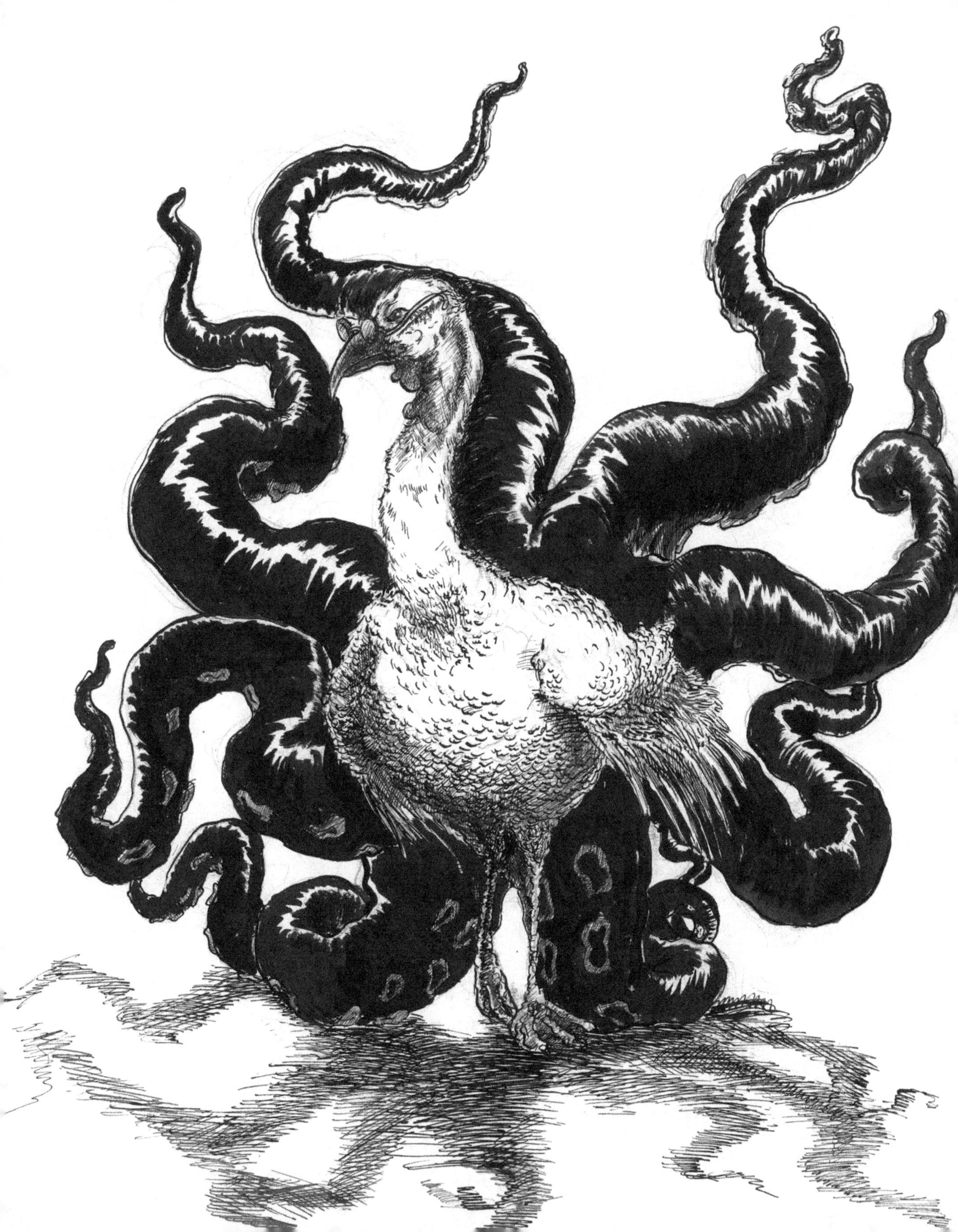

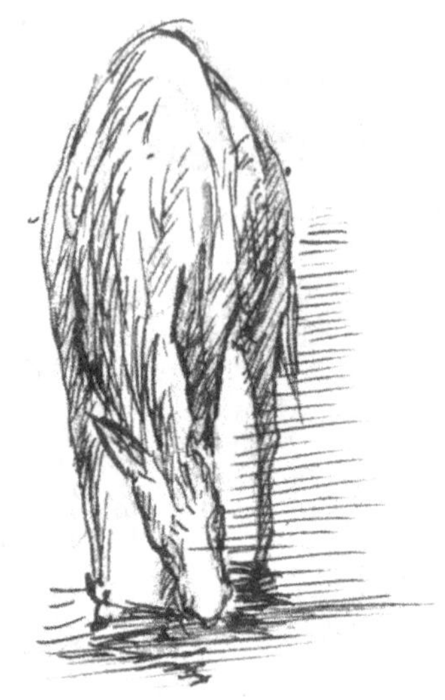

The Horse of a Different Color

Not primary, secondary or even tertiary,
beyond the bounds of reason and all scientific query,
this equine's different color is so outré that it's scary—

unseemly, breaking every rule and yet supremely fair,
it trips the light fantastic, taking logic unaware:
its coat of many colors is a shade beyond compare

and isn't scarlet, crimson, rose, or fire engine red,
nor chartreuse, mint, cerulean, or sapphire blue. Instead
this horse's hue, though bold as brass, is better left unsaid;

for butterflies aren't butterflies once they've been pinned and framed,
and why go see the lions at the circus when they're tamed?
We only seek our dreams at night as long as they're not named.

The Ankylosaurus

Observe this early turtle, one of myriad
herbivores from the Cretaceous Period,
short on intellectual propensity,
since armor's not his only form of density,

who doesn't have a brain, but has a pair,
and isn't very smart, but doesn't care;
which seems a way of thinking that illumines,
given how much thinking does for humans.

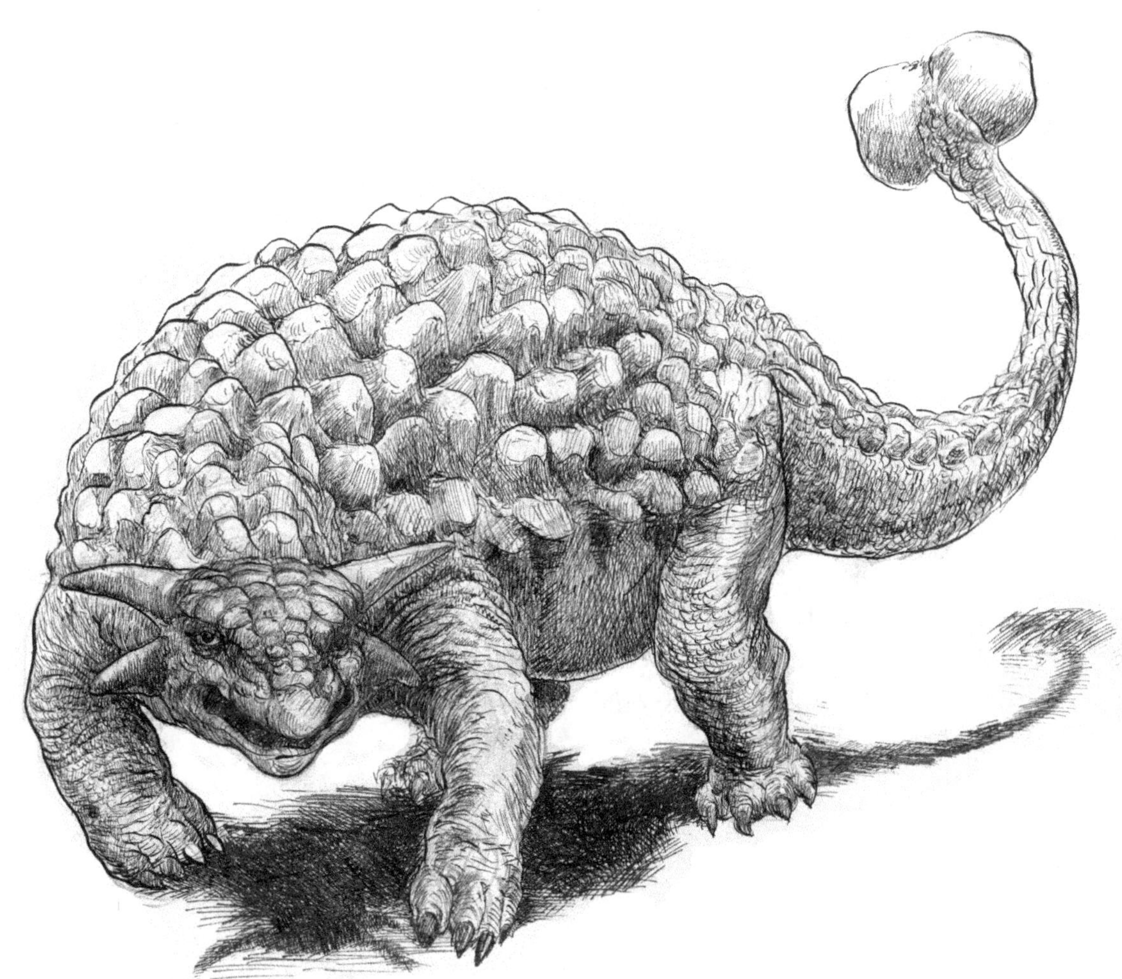

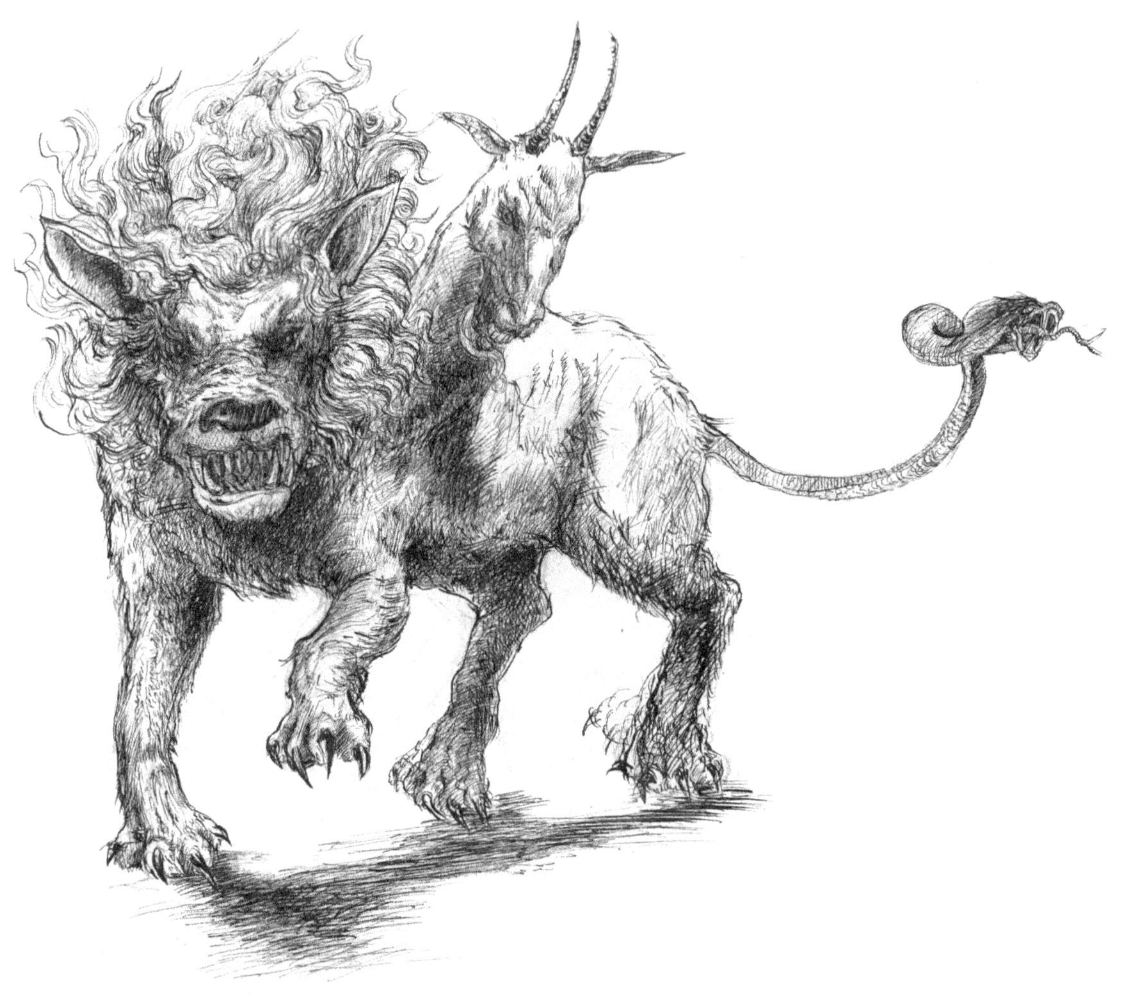

Chimera

That smorgasbord beast, the Chimera,
asked the Egyptian Sphynx, "Is it fair a
goatish head should be fixed
on a creature so mixed?"
She replied, "You should use more mascara."

The Python

The python's painted smirking smile
will widen to a winding mile
of slimy cave that tapers slowly
while prey are slyly swallowed wholly.

Inviting guests to dine within
his empty diamond vault of skin,
this legless devil seems to grovel
before his dark, unfurnished hovel

with eyes like hollow golden charms.
He doesn't seem to carry arms—
then quicker than a man can yell he
proves a python's mostly belly.

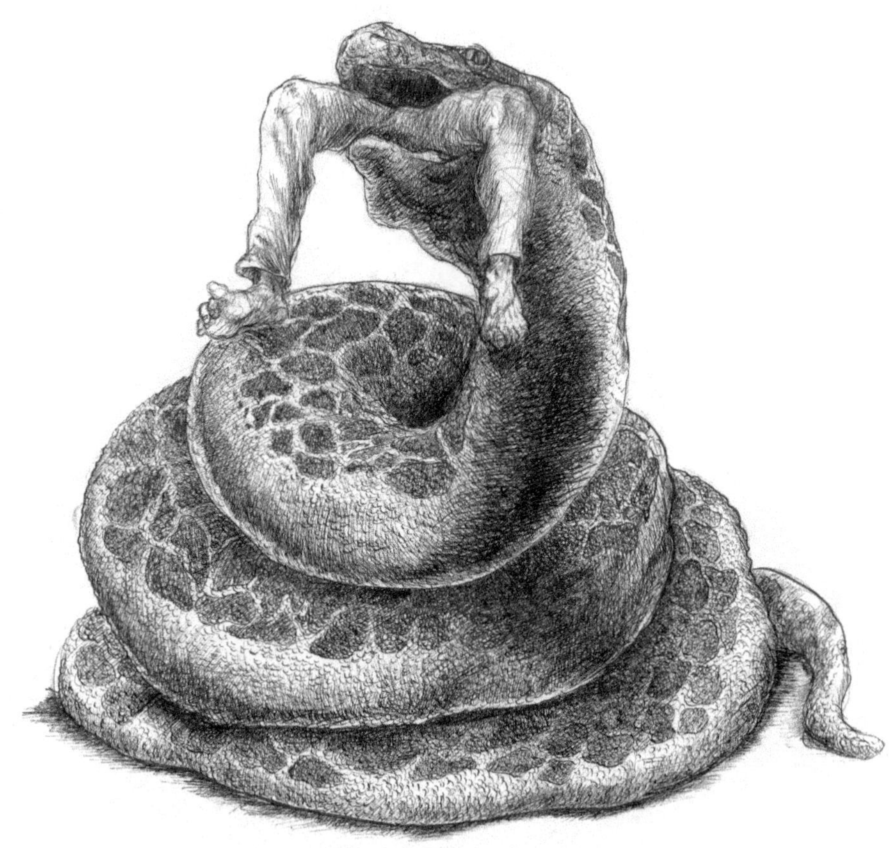

Prey of the Lamia

Half of what you want and half of what
you fear, a dream that snares you half awake,
the Lamia, partly goddess, partly snake,
has coiled as lithely as a hangman's knot

around you, sex upon your sex, her arms
around your neck. Eyes, unblinking, stare
as if the one she's hunted isn't there,
but catch you nonetheless; her gaze, which charms

as cobras charm their prey before they kill,
consumes you and discards you in a game—
she's frozen you and turned you into flame,
burning for a touch too slick and chill:

tonight you are her love who, as she feeds,
the Lamia, partly woman, somewhat needs.

The Heart

It’s wild, and leaps without the “e”—
it wants to touch, to feel, to see:
and though I’m sly, and counted clever,
I cannot keep it caged forever.

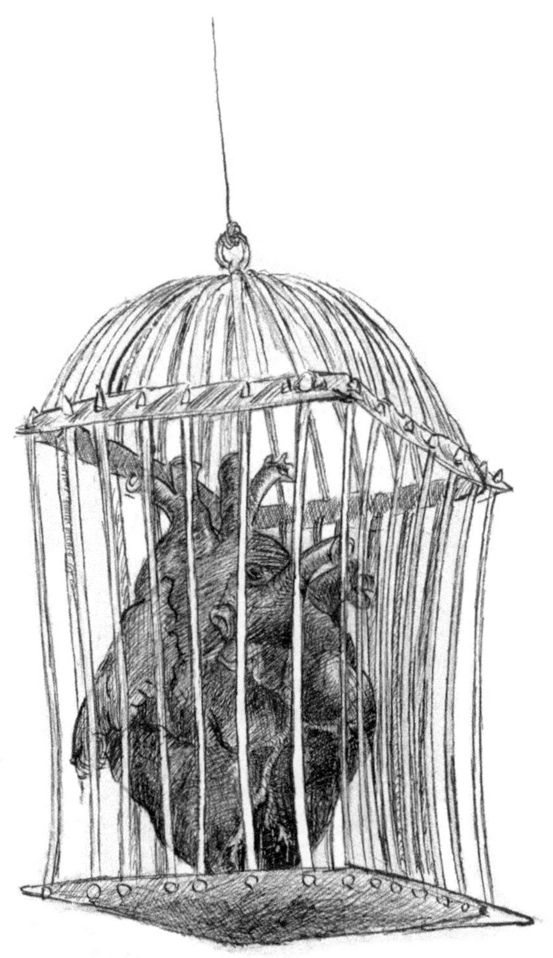

The Friend

What's left is stuffed and mounted, though the wisely pedagogic
insist persistent claims it once existed defy logic—
an artifact encased in glass, astonishing your nieces,
its skull is crushed, its pelt is scalped, its heart is broke to pieces.

They say it stood on battlements and blew its silver horn,
and whistled in the darkest dark before the brightest morn.
It wandered far on camelback with gold, incense, and myrrh.
The Friend would battle with its pack against the Cad and Cur;

but that was all before my time; and yet I've heard the harper
sing if you'll listen quietly, with ears alert, and sharper,
or sit in bars and stand a round, be jolly till the end,
and never think you're wise a lucky man might find a Friend.

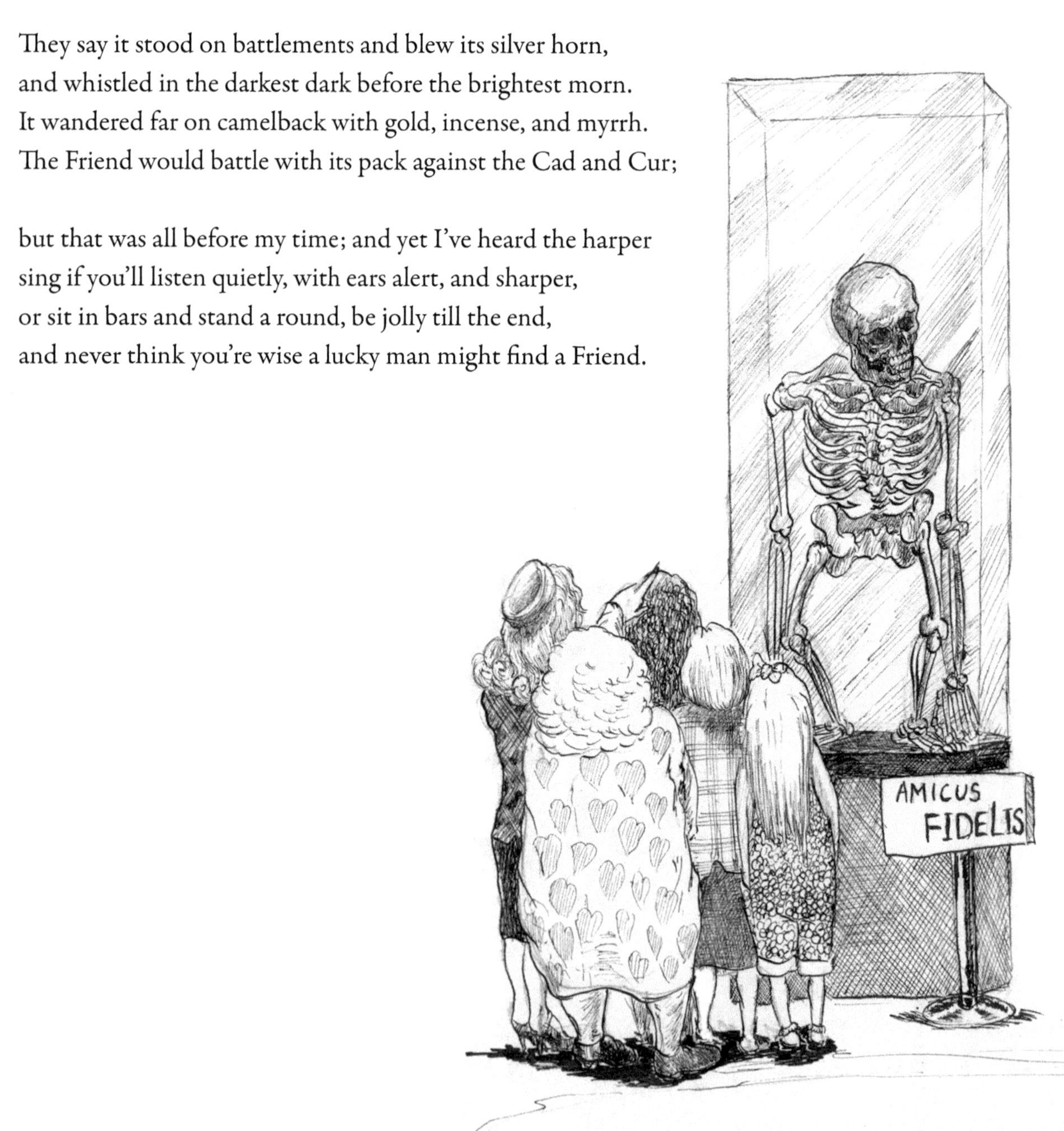

The Cat's Meow

I am the land of the boot to the hat,
the Siamese twin of the Siamese cat.
A swing and a miss, once the boy with the arrows,
a broadened perspective that ages and narrows,

I'm the glare of a window, the smoke from a chimney,
a hound on my trail and a scorpion in me.
I'm the jack in the box. I'm a corpse on a lark,
the length of my shadow, a leap in the dark.

I'm a pearl in an oyster, the kiss of a petal—
the curl of a lip, or the hiss of a kettle.
I'm the treasure that's buried, a little brown penny,
the dog with three heads and a man without any.

I'm a stab in the back and a hand used to shaking,
a dwarf, but a star, and a sleeper awaking,
the home that is sweet and the smile that is sour;
a spider that hides in the face of a flower.

An ink blot on paper, defying analysis,
I'm a beggar whose father is said to own palaces.
Often less, nothing more, I am something like that,
the Siamese twin of the Siamese cat.

The Crocodile

I think when I have made my million
I will become more crocodilian:
my skin will thicken up like armor,
and I'll migrate to someplace warmer,

where those whose hearts are cold are normal,
the eating habits are informal,
and those whose grasps exceed their reaches
loll like logs on lovely beaches.

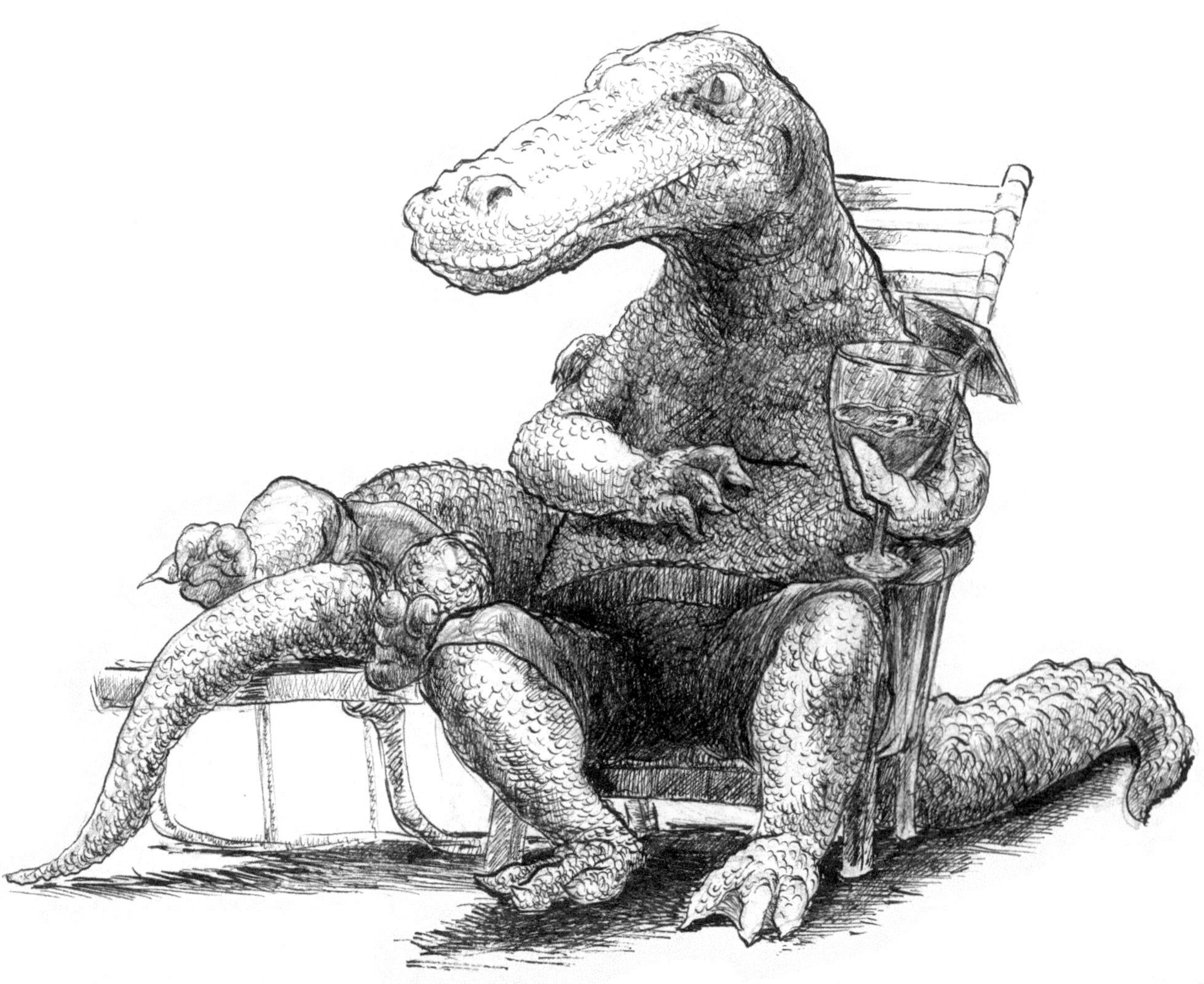

The Flea Circus

I never noticed while the music played
it was a little world a man had made
to fool another little man like you
because the fleas had better things to do.

A Schism of Zebras

Clowns whose camouflage is bold as brass,
but can't disguise how every one's an ass,
they're spry, and rarely captured in *vers libre,*
whose lines can make it hard to find the zibre.

The Antelope

The antelope is springy and superlatively agile,
but frail and fragile,
and—like all who run from their troubles—finds the lion, without question,
has a quicker digestion.

The Kraken

Slimier than earthworms, krakens lend a kind of hand
to sailor boys who've put the boot to castles made of sand,
and roll cheroots from maps with monsters drawn just past the land—

merry lads who climb the masts as nimbly as chimpanzees,
play with knives in quayside dives, get drunk and sing like banshees,
never listing Tennyson among their idle fancies;

who sleep like logs, and wouldn't dream of reaping what they're sowing,
only roamed the halls at school on days they bothered going,
and never studied or engaged in sports, except for rowing.

It's just this sort of boy whose craft will sail without a care
above aphotic grottos where voracious krakens lair,
and find themselves invited to a sumptuous affair:

while children who read Tennyson and heed their parents' wishes
may never hear a mermaid sing, or sleep among the fishes,
but might eat little octopi in cream, which are delicious.

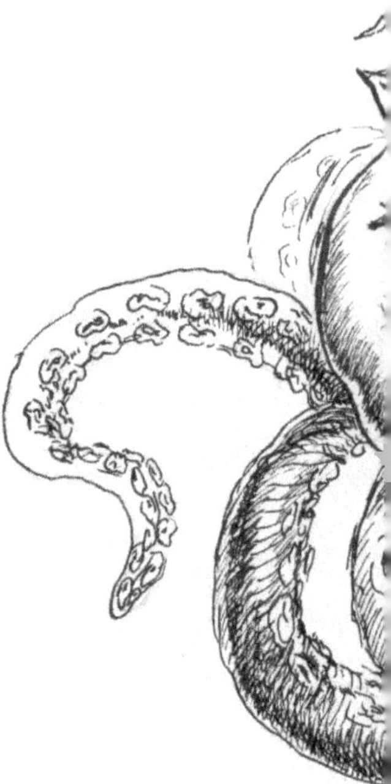

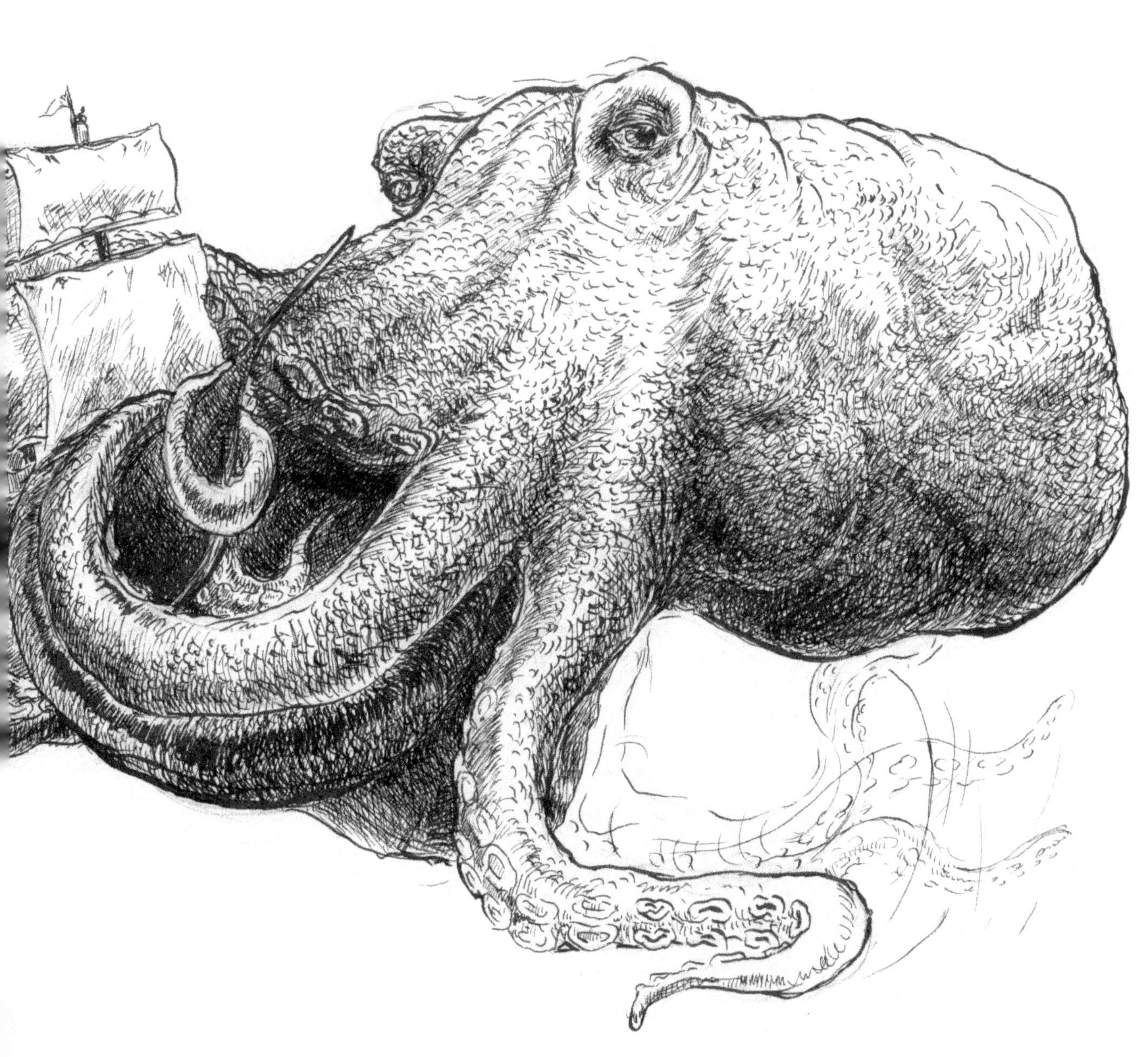

The Logorrhea

Native to the isle of Logor, this mutated rhea
has spread as far as fruit flies, though just why I've no idea;
for most resent its tanned and pleasant, bland, incessant call.
Yet lithe and leggy rheas are my favorite birds of all—

zephyrs of the pampas, as a Paraguayan breeze
flows straight or catawampus though the grass and stunted trees
they gather quietly as clouds, then fade away, like time,
onyx gazes eloquent as gestures by a mime;

so what took place on Logor's wretched isle, just north of Guinea,
to cause this blithe and gentle bird to blither like a ninny,
and warped my finest feathered friends into this yawping choir,
bloviating variants of those infesting Diar?

For now a million gauchos with a hundred million bolas,
the gondoliers of Venice in their fragile dark gondolas,
the Mongol hordes, the army ants, the Aztecs and the Mayans,
the elephants of Hannibal, the lion tamer's lions,

the bulls and bears of Wall Street, English knighthood in its flower,
Bill and all his buffaloes, the hero of the hour,
the cavalry of Custer, legionaries fresh from Rome,
and Davey Crockett couldn't send the Logorrhea home.

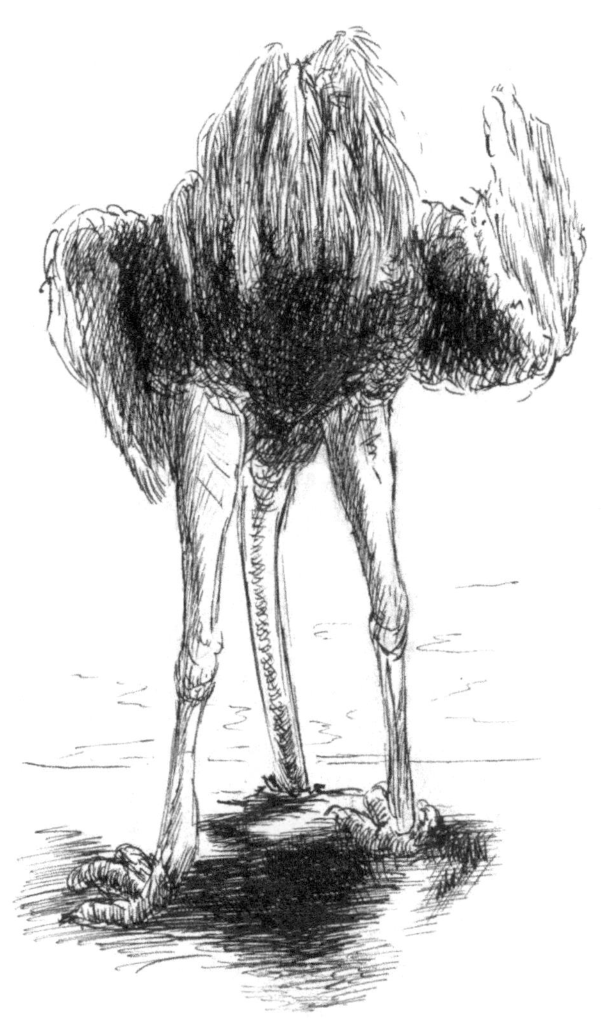

The Ostrich

A feather duster up on stilts
who favors neither pants nor kilts,
he thinks his native state is splendid
and gads about as God intended.

Content with just a hint of wings
and bounty desert living brings,
his mark is light upon the land.
Whose head is buried in the sand?

The Mole People

Blinking like the stars, as deep as night
and ugly as we thought they were, they came,
emerging from clandestine faults to light
abysses surface people feared to name,

and no one saw them coming, as they'd learned
self-effacing insight from the dead.
Untroubled by what common sense discerned,
they looked beyond dark oddities we fled,

and what they were, they were, and didn't hide.
Attempts at dazzlement had no effect,
our offers of enlightenment, denied;
for we who'd not been moved could not direct

the halting, awkward progress of the blind
who felt their way to what we failed to find.

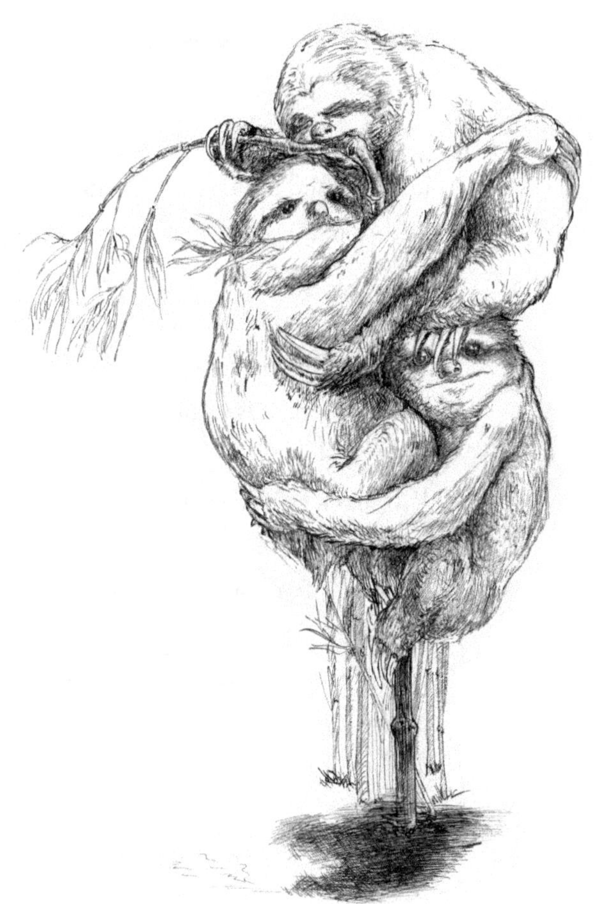

The Sloth

A dilatory brachiator,
abhorring now, adoring later,
the sloth's as slow as carbon dating or
the elevator you've been waiting for.

His limbs are lank, orangutanish;
he holds so still he seems to vanish.
Our days are blurs and blurry, whereas
he takes his ease and thinks in eras.

One vice alone among the seven
has namesakes loafing close to heaven—
for Pride's the prelude to a fall,
Lust, that fire, devours all,

and Gluttony, Envy, Wrath and Greed
make fools of us at greater speed.
Be slothful, then: it wouldn't hurt you
to learn at last which sin's a virtue.

The Picasso Puppy

He thought it was an Easter egg, except it was rectangular,
and lurched about on pipe stem legs, improbable and angular,
with tentacles whose suckered grip was like the Boston Strangular.

He saw a map in red and green tattooed upon its chest
where signs too small for him to read were pointing north and west,
with inky routes to fairyland and islands of the blessed.

Perhaps it was an abacus, perhaps a dictionary,
or else an ice cream sundae with a maraschino cherry,
a gentle downward path with baited traps for the unwary.

Could it be a capybara fresh from Paraguay,
or else a ghost of comedy that haunts a tragic play
whose audience was starved for lines he lacked the wit to say?

It seemed to have a secret name it whispered in his ear:
he whispered back, "I'm sorry, I'm half deaf, and didn't hear."
It sounded like a proverb, but the meaning wasn't clear.

Future tensed and barking mad, it followed him around,
a stray Picasso puppy, framed, but rescued from the pound,
which gibbered like a gibbon, though he couldn't hear a sound—

especially the neighbors, as he felt their fears misplaced
in spite of every gruesome end on which such tales are based;
for he was somewhat monstrous from the terrors he had faced,
and trusted when it licked his hand he wasn't to its taste.

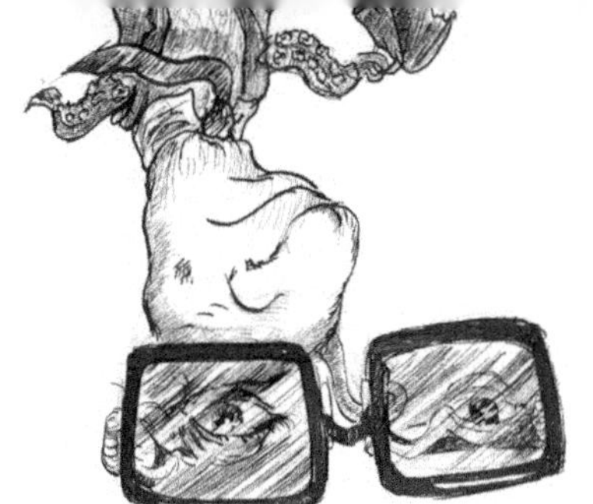

The Snub

Aimed at those it doesn't know but has no cause to fear,
its nose is hypersensitive to things as they appear,
elongated and sloping down at angles most severe.

Oozing social graces while it chooses who to slime,
the Snub will cut you to the quick—it picks the proper time,
then if you're unimportant will invent or find a crime.

A slippery creature made of frost, descended from the Slink,
it skims along the surface, but it won't go near the brink,
equating what's appropriate with what the neighbors think.

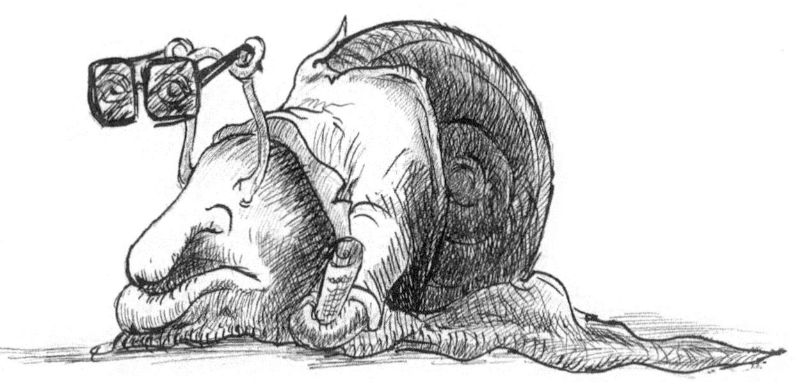

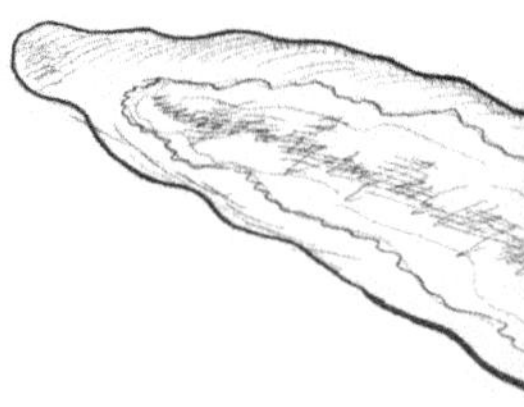

A Fog of Blurbs

Their plumage is a sheen of words whose meanings are the same—
inveigling, too often heard, obnoxious birds, but tame,
their mewling call is pecks of praise without one speck of blame.

Indifferent if they foul their nests or poop rains on the rabble,
garrulously gathered on the garret eaves of Babel,
they preen as they pontificate on arts in which they dabble,

for truth goes out the window when the Blurbs fly into town;
a mist of cloying tidings, thought essential to renown,
their beaks grow long and longer and are uniformly brown.

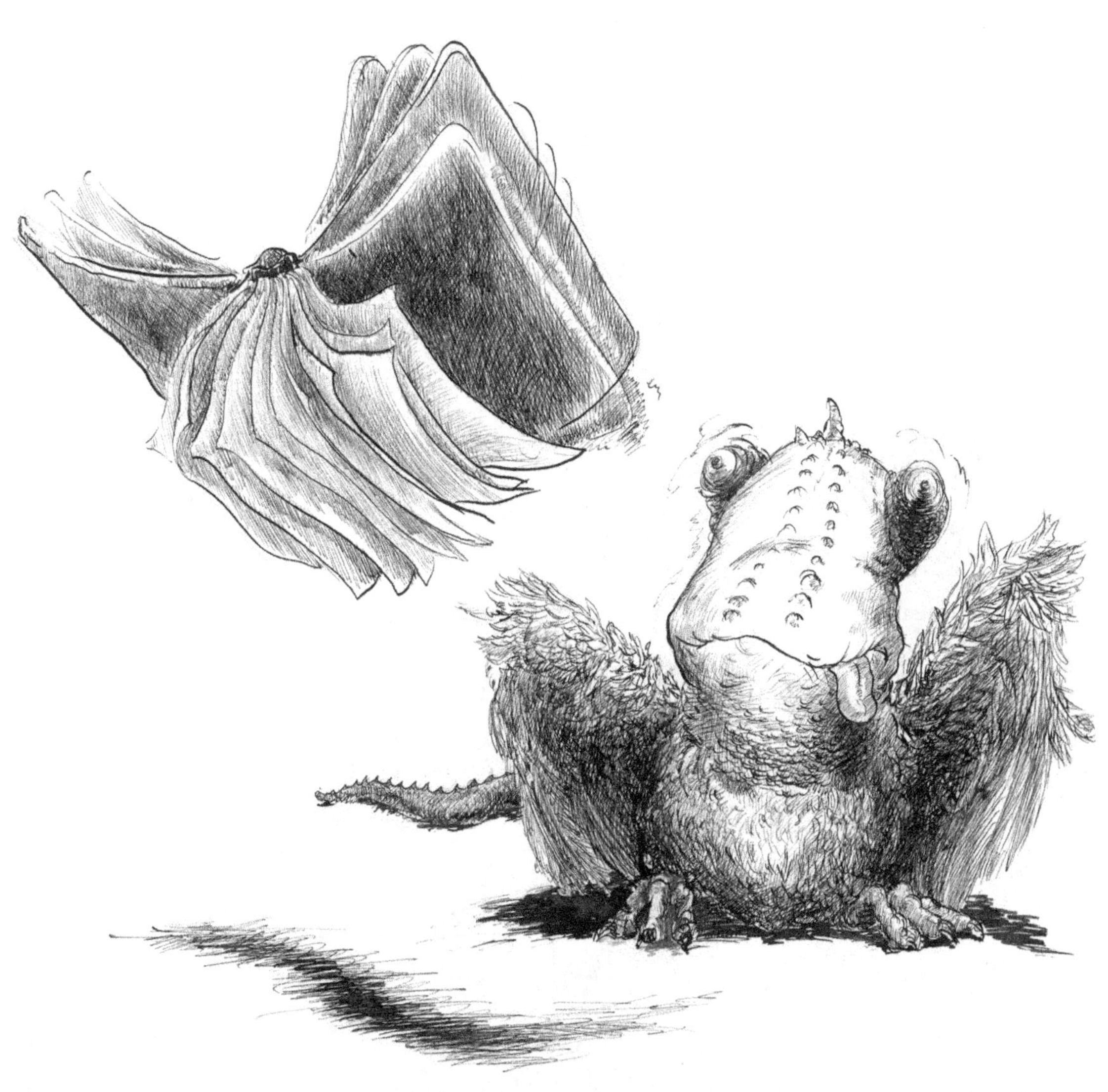

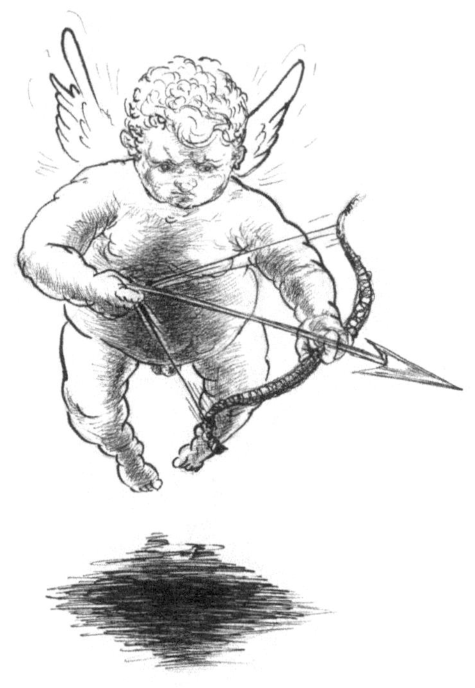

The Winged Boy

The cruel little boy with a bow
who feathers each heart with desires
has missed me so often I know
it hurts more to dodge when he fires.

Song of the Blind Loon

A dark and witchly coven, crows of memory and loss,
plus fiends whose soles are cloven and avow the double cross
are gathered round the oven, having lathered me with sauce.

My childhood dreams lie drunk in bed beside some nameless tart.
My ego's just a shrunken head, the id grows hard of heart,
and like a book debunked, unread, defending abstract art,

or sheep that shirk their herder and abscond beyond the Pale,
my loins forsook their girder to go chasing after tail
while mermaids murmured murder in their hose of golden scale:

and waxing epistolic I have written lovely letters,
played sax while melancholic as I hob-nobbed with my betters,
then watched them bask and frolic with their sailor boys in fetters,

and I have heard them singing each to each but not to me,
so saw no point in clinging to the fancy I was free
as I was blindly winging like a loon above the sea,

for fairies burgle baby teeth, then pack the holes with gauze,
and once I skimmed above the shoals, but now the tide withdraws.
The tempter makes each fool a bed of coals from Santa Claus.

An Aloofness of Snoots

There are two species of the Snoot, the Common and the Rare.
Both smirkly seethe, and lurk beneath veneers of *savoir faire.*
A mobile, upward pest whose nest is egged behind a gate,
the Common's miffed bravado mimics fingernails on slate;

while Rares hunt salmon *canapés* with slender silver spoons
and lair in fine department stores on Sunday afternoons.
The two will spat like dogs and cats, or Rivendell and Mordor.
They're prone to murder for ascendance in the pecking order.

The Lion and the Unicorn have nothing on the Snoot
for fighting over nothing and for making much of moot
with poison dripping from each glance, their nostrils in the air.
Go gingerly about the Snoot, the Common and the Rare.

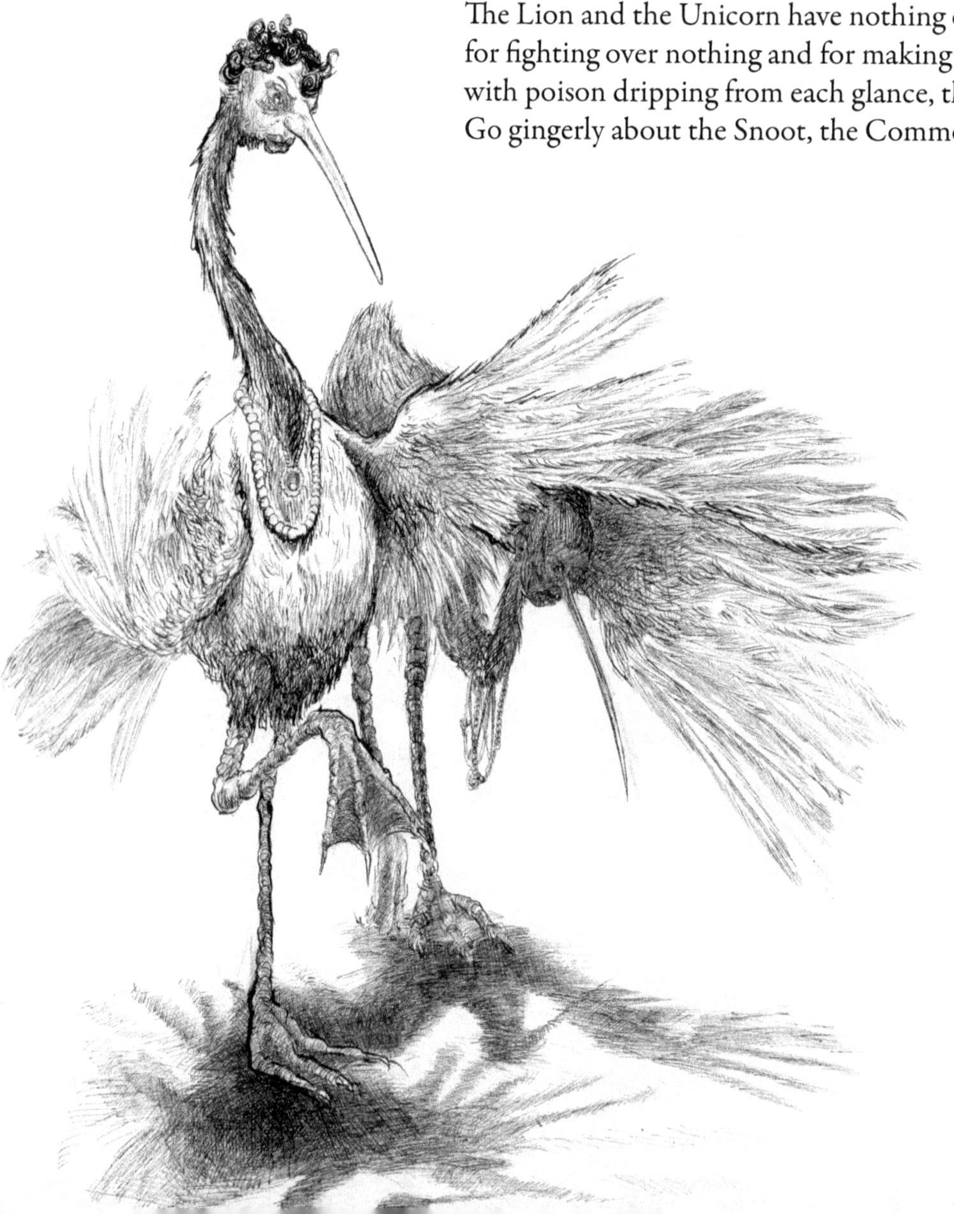

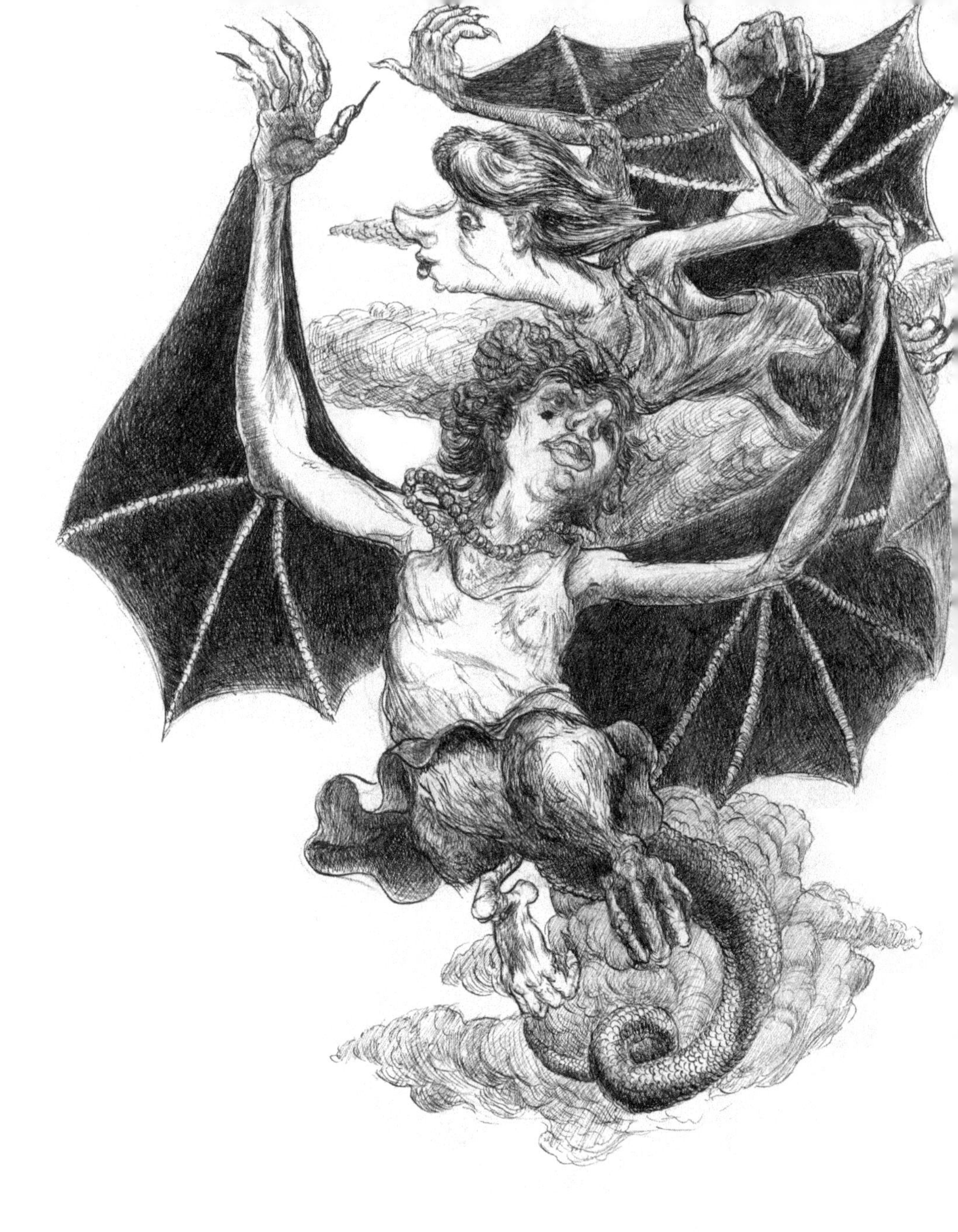

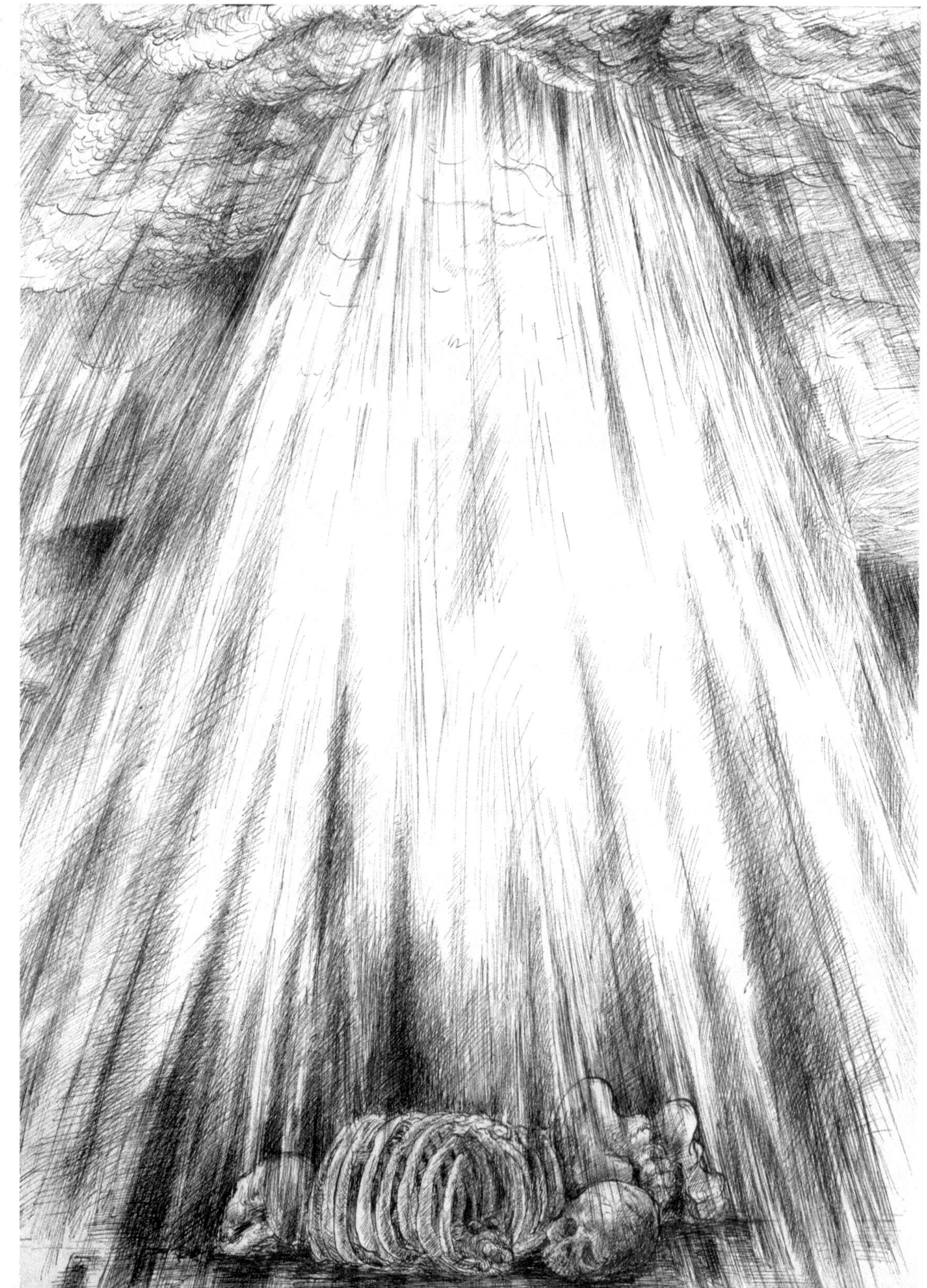

So We Beat Them

One limped a little, and another had a stammer,
one was cross-eyed, swarthy, and employed atrocious grammar;
so we beat them with a pipe, and then a club, and then a plier,
bending them like pretzels after binding them with wire,
sending trite condolences with tappings of a hammer.

One was far too clever, another drolly thick,
one was hyper, one disfigured by a nervous tic;
so we beat them with a tire iron, then aimed a rolling pin
at tender ribs, boxed their ears, and kicked them in the shin,
pretending we were sorry while we plied the heavy stick.

A fear of heights gripped one; one lived in mother's cellar;
one, depressed, developed gout and had a pasty pallor;
so we beat them in a mixing bowl till minds were scrambled eggs,
safe and snug at home because we'd manacled their legs,
and lent our ears but didn't hear their squalls amid the squalor.

One ignored the hoi polloi as they were mouthing curses,
one kept her nose in books and mumbled antiquated verses;
so we beat them with the crucifix, an ankh, and shepherd's crooks,
painted them like prison walls and hoisted them on hooks,
and pent them on their merry way in gilded, garish hearses:

and when they got to heaven with its lovely rolling beaches,
their uniforms restarched and blanched to white with holy bleaches,
we beat them with a lightning rod, the hand of God, and thunder,
for only strikes against the flint can spark a soul to wonder.
There is no balm in Gilead but serpent oil and leeches.

Worms in the End

He let his shadow slip the leash to give his stretch some room,
and taught his future how to fetch. He switched his who to whom,
climbing social ladders and then lowering the boom.

Lowing in the meadow, cows about to stalk the corn
believed the greenest ghetto would receive the ripest morn,
and just like them he said, "O Bluest Boy, come blue your horn,

"for blues are what I feel inside—or like to say I do
while chatting up my neighbors as I'm knocking back a brew.
Living high upon the hog, we love the swinish view."

When angels snuck him cakes or manna freshly baked by God,
he'd mock their stale hosannas, while presuming they'd applaud
his quest amid banana peels Fate littered on the sod;

yet finishing ahead, he found, was neck and neck with last.
A dirty blanket round him with the earthworms swimming past,
he reached the Desk of No Returns, and learned his die was cast.

They strapped him in the judgment seat, a wooden single seater.
"Who taught my shadow how to fetch?" the shade kvetched, while Peter
lounged behind the desk—serene, but frowning at the meter.

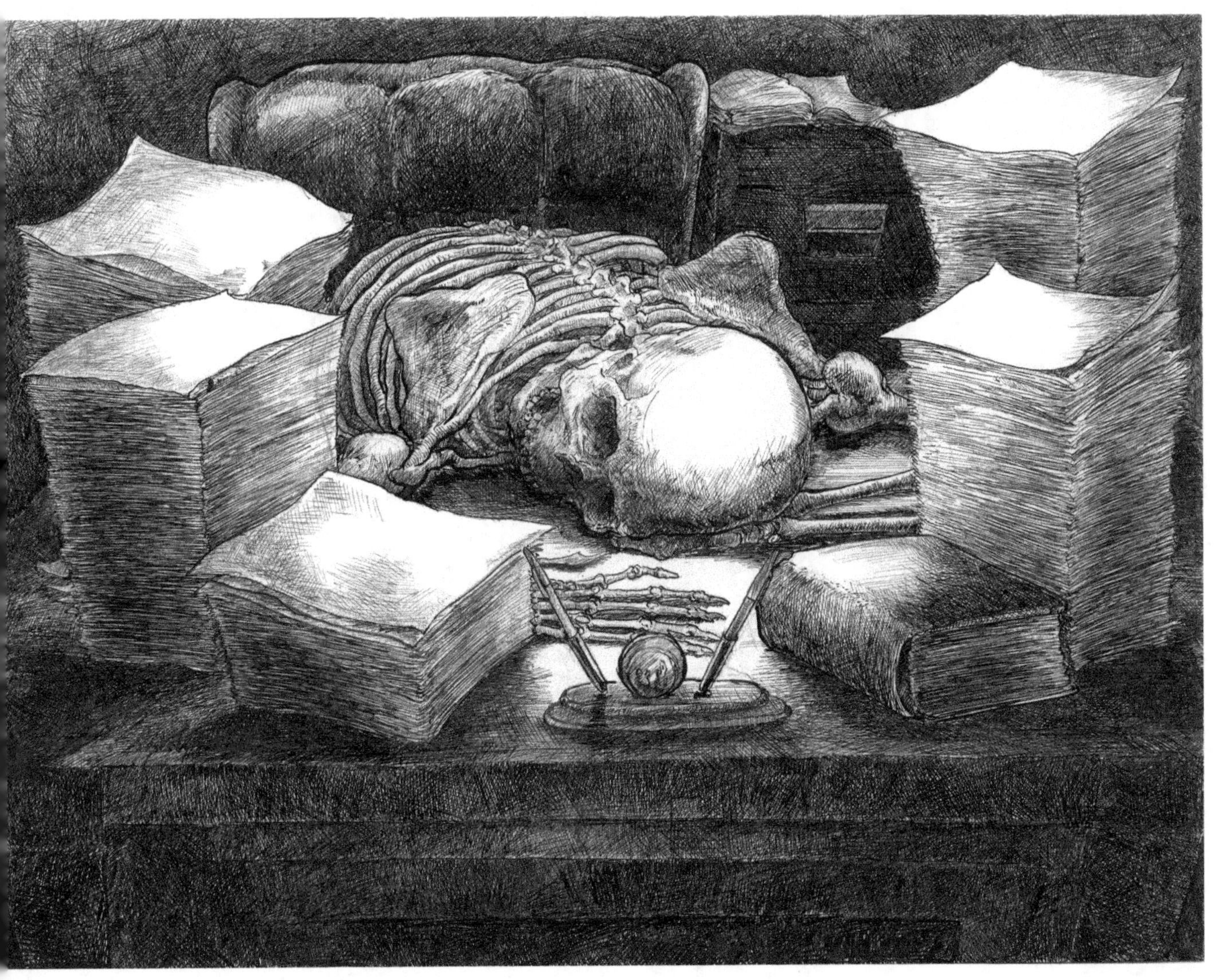

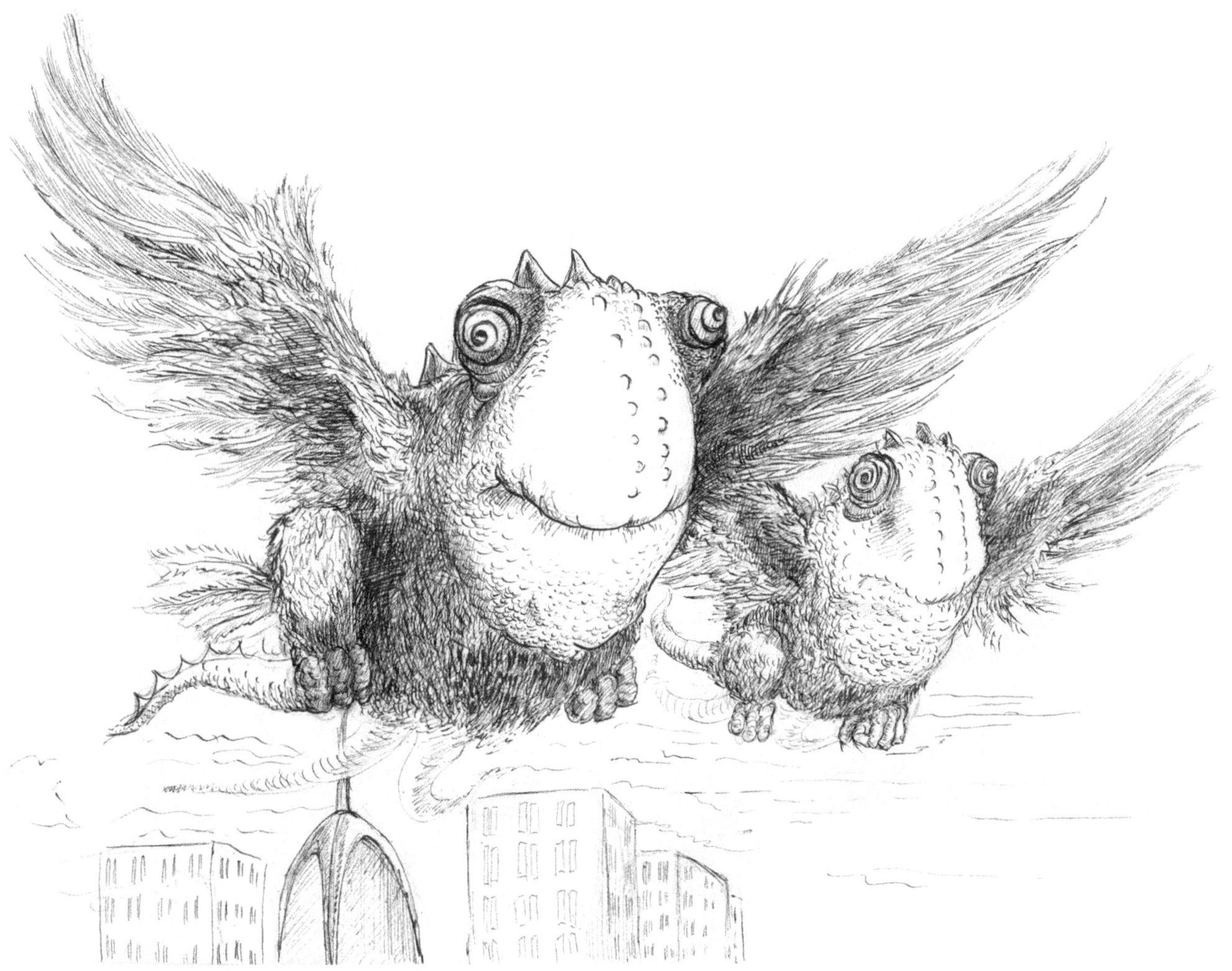

A Mist of Cloying Tidings

"With the serrated delicacy of ghoulish medical students at the height of their powers, Shacklee and Spitkovsky plumb the brooding, fecund underbellies of postmodern American thought."—*The Erewhon Quarterly*

"Informed by a felicitous empathy, bristling with haunting delight, Spitkovsky's deftly incendiary art is a sovereign remedy for dormant, volcanic ills."—*Drawn Quarterly*

"Strikingly aboriginal, the palimpsestic sparkle of Shacklee's wit illumines a Sisyphean ascent, boldly endeavored through goat-footed epiphanies."—*The French Quarter Picayune*

"As if Kafka's castle was brilliantly reimagined as a miniature golf course, or Thackeray's *Vanity Fair* was stuffed into a sack full of kittens and thrown off a bridge, *The Blind Loon*'s scantily clad muse lures with a frumious jingle. Each darkly light, lyric romp is executed with a Pyrrhic triumph."—*Qatar: A Journal of Quarterly Verse*

Ed Shacklee, whose poetry has appeared in the *Able Muse, Light,* and *Rattle* among other journals, is a public defender who represents young people. He lives on a boat in the Potomac River.
The *Blind Loon* is his first full-length collection.

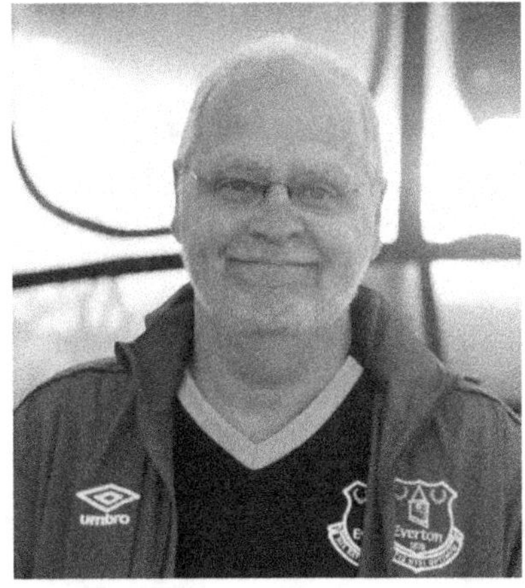

Also from Able Muse Press

William Baer, *Times Square and Other Stories*

Lee Harlin Bahan, *A Year of Mourning (Petrarch) – Translation*

Melissa Balmain, *Walking in on People – Poems*

Ben Berman, *Strange Borderlands – Poems*

Ben Berman, *Figuring in the Figure – Poems*

Michael Cantor, *Life in the Second Circle – Poems*

Catherine Chandler, *Lines of Flight – Poems*

William Conelly, *Uncontested Grounds – Poems*

Maryann Corbett, *Credo for the Checkout Line in Winter – Poems*

Maryann Corbett, *Street View – Poems*

John Philip Drury, *Sea Level Rising – Poems*

D.R. Goodman, *Greed: A Confession – Poems*

Margaret Ann Griffiths, *Grasshopper – The Poetry of M A Griffiths*

Katie Hartsock, *Bed of Impatiens – Poems*

Elise Hempel, *Second Rain – Poems*

Jan D. Hodge, *Taking Shape – carmina figurata*

Jan D. Hodge, *The Bard & Scheherazade Keep Company – Poems*

Ellen Kaufman, *House Music – Poems*

Carol Light, *Heaven from Steam – Poems*

April Lindner, *This Bed Our Bodies Shaped – Poems*

Martin McGovern, *Bad Fame – Poems*

Jeredith Merrin, *Cup – Poems*

Richard Newman, *All the Wasted Beauty of the World – Poems*

Alfred Nicol, *Animal Psalms – Poems*

Frank Osen, *Virtue, Big as Sin – Poems*

Alexander Pepple (Editor), *Able Muse Anthology*

Alexander Pepple (Editor),
Able Muse – a review of poetry, prose & art
(semiannual issues, Winter 2010 onward)

James Pollock, *Sailing to Babylon – Poems*

Aaron Poochigian, *The Cosmic Purr – Poems*

Aaron Poochigian, *Manhattanite – Poems*

John Ridland, *Sir Gawain and the Green Knight – Translation*

Stephen Scaer, *Pumpkin Chucking – Poems*

Hollis Seamon, *Corporeality – Stories*

Carrie Shipers, *Embarking on Catastrophe – Poems*

Matthew Buckley Smith, *Dirge for an Imaginary World – Poems*

Barbara Ellen Sorensen,
Compositions of the Dead Playing Flutes – Poems

Wendy Videlock, *Slingshots and Love Plums – Poems*

Wendy Videlock, *The Dark Gnu and Other Poems*

Wendy Videlock, *Nevertheless – Poems*

Richard Wakefield, *A Vertical Mile – Poems*

Gail White, *Asperity Street – Poems*

Chelsea Woodard, *Vellum – Poems*

www.ablemusepress.com

www.ingramcontent.com/pod-product-compliance
Lightning Source LLC
LaVergne TN
LVHW080331110826
845155LV00024B/147